# Celtic
# Myths

*For Elisabeth*

## Picture credits

THE · LEGENDARY · PAST

# Celtic

# Myths

## MIRANDA JANE GREEN

Published in cooperation with
BRITISH MUSEUM PRESS
UNIVERSITY OF TEXAS PRESS, AUSTIN

Third University of Texas Press edition, 1998

ISBN 0–292–72754–2
Library of Congress Catalog Card Number 93–60590

Designed by Gill Mouqué
Cover design by Slatter-Anderson
Printed in Great Britain by The Bath Press, Avon

FRONT COVER *The Snettisham gold torc, first century AD, now in the British Museum.*

THIS PAGE *Stone horse-head frieze from the early Celtic shrine of Roquepertuse, southern France, fifth–fourth century BC. Musée Borély, Marseille.*

# Contents

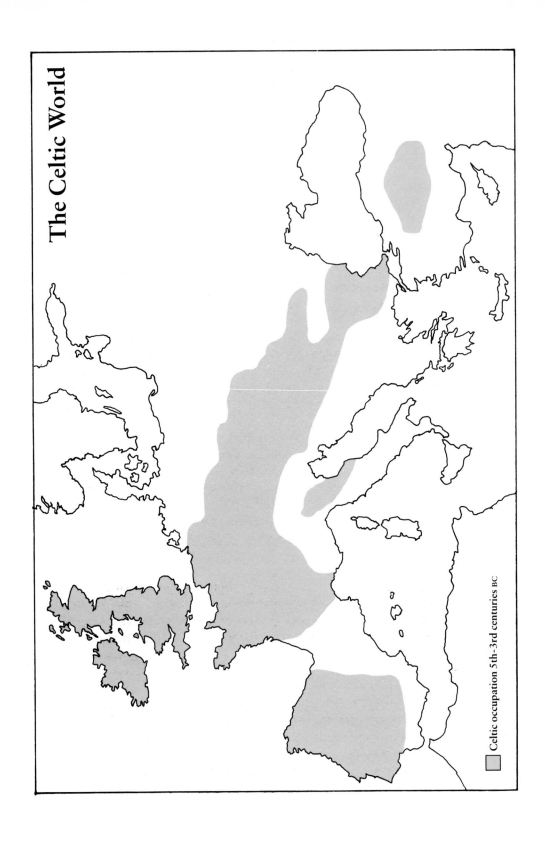

The Celtic World

Celtic occupation 5th–3rd centuries BC

# How do we know about Celtic myths?

What do we mean by 'myth' and 'mythology'? These are flexible terms with a variety of meanings. For me myths are inextricably associated with religion. A useful definition involves the perception of a myth as a symbolic story, similar to a parable, a means by which human imagination can express a concept whose meaning is too complex and profound to be conveyed by simple verbal messages. In this way myths can deal with fundamental issues such as who we are, why we exist, what happens when we die: universal concerns which are unanswerable in terms of the rational explanations born of human experience. Myths can explain the phenomena of the natural world – the behaviour of the sun, weather, drought and flood – in terms of the super-natural. Thus myths exist by virtue of their link with the divine and with cult. They contain traditions of sacred beings – gods and heroes – and their association with mortals, which contribute to the framework of belief-systems. In this book the stories themselves, as they exist in the vernacular traditions of Ireland and Wales, form the fundamental core of myth in its strictest sense. But to my mind, because myths are so closely linked with religion, it is equally important to examine the other evidence for Celtic belief-systems, namely the chroniclings of the Classical writers and the archaeological material.

## Time and space

*Celtic Myths* sets out to explore the mythology and beliefs of the pagan Celts between about 600 BC and AD 400, although some of the evidence cited in the book falls outside this range. At the period of maximum expansion (fifth–third centuries BC) the Celtic world occupied an area from Ireland and part of Spain in the west to Hungary and Czechoslovakia in the east (but including Galatia in Asia Minor), and from northern Scotland to north Italy and what was formerly Yugoslavia. Mediterranean authors first speak of *Keltoi* about 500 BC and it is then, or even earlier, that archaeologists can distinguish a certain homogeneity in material culture over much of Europe north of the Alps. From the third century BC, Celtic place-names and personal names endorse this geographical distribution of Celtic peoples.

There is no clear-cut boundary between the end of paganism and the beginning of Christianity in Celtic Europe. The old gods lingered long, but during the fourth century AD Christianity was officially adopted as the state religion by the Roman world, and in Britain and Ireland, where Celtic traditions were arguably sustained longest, the Celtic Church was established during the fifth century AD.

## The problem of finding Celtic myths

The main difficulty in reaching Celtic myth and religion is that the pagan Celts were virtually non-literate and therefore did not describe their beliefs and their attitudes to the supernatural world in writing. This means that all our evidence is, in a real sense, indirect. That which exists falls into three categories, between which there are tensions and contradictions and all of which have, to a degree, to be treated separately: the chronicles of contemporary commentators from the Classical world; the later vernacular documents of Ireland and Wales; and the archaeology.

## The evidence of the Classical commentators

Observers from the Greek and Roman world commented on the traditions, cults and rituals of their northern, 'barbarian' neighbours. Their testimony has the value of contemporaneity but it has inherent problems of bias, distortion, misunderstanding and omission. Unlike the Celts these observers belonged to a culture in which cities played an important role and, indeed, were regarded as the key to civilisation. Alongside rural and private cults, Mediterranean culture possessed an organised state religious system, based upon these urban centres. Thus Classical commentators on the Celts were witnesses to a set of traditions and thought-processes which were alien to them and which were based upon a less sophisticated religion. So there is the danger that Mediterranean authors selected and sensationalised aspects of cult-behaviour which they felt would fit the image of a primitive people, beyond the edge of the civilised world. Certainly the picture painted by these writers is very fragmentary. There is little information about divine beings and, where it does occur – as in the case of Caesar's chronicles – there is confusion and sometimes spurious equation between Celtic and Roman deities, and Celtic religion is frequently perceived according to the framework of the Graeco-Roman world.

Many Classical writers make some allusion to Celtic religion. A main source was Posidonius, a Greek philosopher of the Stoic School, whose first-century BC writings are lost but whose observations were quarried by a number of later commentators. Our main sources are Caesar (writing in the mid-first century BC); Strabo (late first century BC–early first century AD); Diodorus Siculus (writing c. 60–30 BC); Lucan (first century AD) and Dio Cassius (later second–early third century AD). Between them they present a large body of evidence mainly concerning ritual practices: druidism, divination, human sacrifice and head-hunting. They also comment on the Celtic attitude to death and the Otherworld (the perception of life after death as similar to that of earth).

What is missing is any clear picture of a Celtic pantheon or belief-system.

Occasionally we can discern links between these ancient documents and other sources of evidence. Thus the divinatory powers of the druids are chronicled in the early Insular (Irish) tradition. Classical writers, archaeology and the earliest Celtic stories all bear witness to the importance of water-cults; the religious significance of the human head; and a strong belief in life after death.

## The vernacular sources

The earliest stories written in Irish and Welsh contain a large body of material which pertains to a Celtic mythological tradition. We use these stories, and not the early archaeological record, as our starting point for discussion since they are the sources most familiar to modern readers interested in Celtic mythology. However, this category of evidence has to be approached with caution if any attempt is made to link the myths and constant allusions to the supernatural world in this literature to the world of the pagan Celts as defined by archaeology or the Classical documents. First, the vernacular sources are late in their extant form and, moreover, they were compiled within a Christian milieu, many of them by Christian redactors, monks working within monasteries. Second, these writings relate specifically and solely to Wales and Ireland, which were on the western periphery of the Celtic world during the pagan Celtic period.

### Ireland

The Irish oral tradition began first to be preserved in written form during the sixth century AD. However, the majority of the surviving manuscripts date from no earlier than the twelfth century. Their value lies in their undoubted inclusion of material which relates to a much earlier phase of Irish settlement, perhaps referring as far back as the pagan period: that is, before the fifth century AD.

There are three collections of Irish prose tales which are especially relevant to the Celtic world of the supernatural. One is the 'Mythological Cycle', which includes the *Leabhar Gabhála* or *Book of Invasions*, and the *Dinnshenchas* or *History of Places*, both compiled in the twelfth century AD. The *Book of Invasions* has its origins in much earlier compilations of monastic scholars constructing a 'History of Ireland' in the sixth and seventh centuries AD. It describes a succession of mythical invasions of Ireland from before the Flood, culminating in the coming of the Gaels or Celts. Its purpose seems to have been to establish a Myth of Creation, an explanation of the nature of Ireland and the presence of the Celts. The 'invasion' of greatest interest in the present context is that of the Tuatha Dé Danann, the divine race of Ireland, who consisted of numerous gods and goddesses, each with particular functions and concerns. The *Dinnshenchas* is less useful, but it comprises a collection of topographical lore, in which the names of places are explained in terms of myth.

The second group of tales is contained in the Ulster Cycle, of which the most important form a collection of stories known as the *Táin Bó Cuailnge* (the *Cattle Raid of Cooley*). This chronicles the great conflict between the two most northerly of the five ancient provinces of Ulster and Connacht. The *Táin* is steeped in the supernatural: Ulster is peopled by superhuman heroes, such as Cú Chulainn, and by druids, such as Cathbadh; Connacht is ruled by a euhemerised (i.e. a divine being perceived as a historical figure) queen-goddess, Medb; and the destiny of the two kingdoms rests in the hands of the great war- and death-goddesses, the Morrigán and the Badbh. The Ulster Cycle, as its name suggests, is a mythological tradition which belongs only to Ulster; there is nothing comparable for any other region of Ireland. Part of the earliest-known form of the *Táin* is contained within a flawed and fragmentary text in the oldest manuscript, called the *Leabhar na h Uidre* or *Book of the Dun Cow*. This was compiled in the twelfth century at the Monastery of Clonmacnois. In origin, however, the *Táin* is much older: the language of the earliest form of the story belongs to the eighth century, but many scholars believe some passages to be several centuries earlier still, although others challenge this view.

The third group of relevant stories is found within the 'Fionn Cycle', again compiled in the twelfth century. It contains less material of relevance to a study of myth, but it chronicles the activities of the hero Finn and his heroic war-band, the Fianna, all of whom are of supernatural status. The interest of these stories lies in their close affinity with the natural world and in the supernatural creatures which inhabit it. This animistic attitude to the world is a tradition for which close parallels can be found in the archaeological evidence for Celtic religion.

There is a great deal of controversy as to the value of the early Insular (Irish) sources in contributing to a construction of Celtic mythology. Not only were they compiled in the medieval period and within a Christian context, but the language used often suggests that the stories were produced no earlier than the eighth century. Indeed some of the descriptions themselves are strongly indicative of medieval Ireland. It is dangerously speculative to make close links between Irish epic literature and the pagan Celtic society chronicled by Classical writers. The gap in space and time between the Celtic Europe of the later first millennium BC and the Ireland of the early historical period is too great a gulf to ignore. But there is, nonetheless, incontrovertible evidence that some of the Irish material contains records of a Celtic tradition that is pre-Christian. This archaism is especially apparent in the Ulster Cycle, which describes a situation prior to the fifth century AD when Ulster's political position within Ireland fundamentally changed. The early, pre-Christian, political organisation encapsulated here is explicable in terms of the function of the compilers, which was to chronicle the past. There are other factors which point to pagan origins. Christianity is not apparent in these Insular legends, and a world is described whose perception of the supernatural belongs to a pre-Christian tradition.

Whatever the date the tales were compiled, they contain much that is pagan and mythological. Even so, there are genuine problems if attempts are made to link the written myths with the archaeological evidence for pagan Celtic religion, although some concepts, such as the sacred power of 'three' are prominent in both sources. While the personalities of Celtic divinities are

*This Romano-Celtic stone relief from Cirencester, Gloucestershire, shows three genii cucullati (little hooded gods of fertility and well-being).*

present in the literature, no allusion is made to the forms of worship or the belief-systems associated with them. With very few exceptions it is impossible to make direct identification between the gods of the Tuatha Dé Danann and the deities whose names were recorded on inscriptions in the early first millennium AD. The name of the Irish god Nuadu may be philologically linked with Nodens, whose large sanctuary on the River Severn was erected in the third century AD, and there are other examples of possible connections, but they are rare indeed. The problem with the Insular material could result from Christian 'laundering' of pagan tradition, whereby redactors who were either ignorant of or hostile to Irish paganism may have deliberately redefined or restructured the world of the supernatural in order to neutralise it. Thus Celtic religion is diluted and all that is left are superhuman heroes or gods who have been cut off from their original theological systems.

## Wales

The early Welsh vernacular tradition contains elements of a rich mythology, but it is poorly documented compared to that of Ireland, and it shows evidence of greater modification from later stories. God is invoked constantly and the great array of pagan divinities seen, for example, in the Irish *Book of Invasions*, is nowhere present in the Welsh tradition. It is also possible to observe that international story-motifs are interleaved within the early Welsh material. There are links, too, between the mythological traditions of Wales and the Continental cycle of medieval Arthurian romance. The Welsh Arthur is a hero, who champions causes and braves the Otherworld in the thirteenth-century poem in the Book of Taliesin, the *Spoils of Annwn*.

Little in the extant Welsh manuscripts is demonstrably early enough for us to make direct links between the myths of Wales and the religion of the pagan Celts. So these myths can make, at best, a limited contribution to the construction of a pagan Celtic cult-system. The Welsh mythology is present but it has largely been reshaped within a different context, so that it is often barely recognisable as myth. The most relevant and the earliest material is contained within the *Pedair Ceinc y Mabinogi*, the *Four Branches of the Mabinogi* (sometimes known as the *Mabinogion*) and the *Tale of Culhwch and Olwen*, together with other material such as *The Dream of Rhonabwy* and *Peredur*. *Culhwch and Olwen* is perhaps the earliest of the mythological Welsh stories, dating to the tenth century in its original form. The *Mabinogi* was first compiled later, in the eleventh century. The early Welsh tradition is preserved in two collections: the *White Book of Rhydderch*, written in about 1300, and the *Red Book of Hergest*, which dates to the later fourteenth century. Much of the subject-matter both of *Culhwch and Olwen* and the *Four Branches* appears to relate to traditions which belong to earlier centuries than the ones in which they were compiled in their present form.

All the tales chronicle the activities of euhemerised supernatural beings whose divinity is not overt but is betrayed by their physical and moral stature. The myths of Wales abound in enchanted or magical animals; metamorphosis from human to animal form; heads with divine properties; and cauldrons capable of resurrecting the dead. There is a pagan Underworld, Annwn, presided over by Arawn, perceived as similar to life on earth and indeed very akin to the Otherworld described in the Irish tradition.

As with the Irish myths it is difficult to make other than tenuous links between Welsh myth and pagan Celtic religion as evidenced by archaeology. Occasionally Welsh beings may be directly related to Celtic divinities: Mabon the Hunter in *Culhwch and Olwen* is surely the Maponus of Romano-Celtic dedications in north Britain and Gaul. The supernatural qualities of cauldrons, human heads and animals are very close to the religious traditions which may be observed in the material culture of the pagan Celts. In addition there are some direct links between the Irish and the Welsh myths: shape-changing, animal-affinities, magical cauldrons exemplify this commonality of tradition.

## The archaeological evidence

The main category of evidence which pertains directly to the pagan Celtic period is that of archaeology, the study of the material culture of Celtic religion: sanctuaries and sacred space; burial customs; ritual behaviour; epigraphy; and iconography (imagery, as portrayed in, for instance, sculpture, figurines or coins). This group of evidence has its own inherent difficulties: archaeologists can deal only with what has survived and, in addition, there are bound to be real problems associated with the interpretation of the thoughts and beliefs of communities who lived 2000 years ago solely from material remains of those beliefs. The other major problem with the archaeological evidence is that much of the iconography relating to Celtic religion dates from the time of Roman influence on Celtic lands, thereby making it difficult to disentangle Celtic symbolism and belief from the Roman tradition with which it became so closely intertwined.

The relevant archaeological evidence encompasses a period when Celts can first be distinguished by their material culture (*c*. seventh–sixth centuries

*The famous gilt-silver cauldron from Gundestrup, Denmark. Second-first century BC.*

BC) until the official demise of Celtic paganism, which is roughly coeval with the end of the Roman occupation of Celtic lands (around AD 400).

There is substantive archaeological evidence for pre-Roman Celtic religious space (see 'Druids, sacrifice and ritual', page 66–7). Built shrines did exist, although these did not conform to a formalised religious architecture. But sacred space often consisted of open-air enclosures, holy lakes, woods and springs. The Celts also dug deep pits or shafts in order to communicate with the powers of the Underworld. There is evidence, too, of repeated and formalised activity which has no apparent functional purpose and therefore may, with some confidence, be termed 'ritual behaviour'. This includes votive deposition in watery contexts, the ritual destruction of offerings, and sacrifice of living things.

In the 'free' or pre-Roman Celtic world there were relatively few stone or metal images of the gods (although the chance preservation of wooden objects leads us to believe that these may have been relatively common). Before the introduction of Graeco-Roman influences, resulting in a rich blend of intrusive and indigenous religious traditions which have left abundant material traces in the archaeological record, evidence of a Celtic belief-system is inconclusive. Celtic art was concerned more with the production of abstract design than with

13

figural and overtly religious imagery. But there are some examples of free Celtic stone iconography in the form of reliefs and statues, the earliest dating to the sixth–fifth centuries BC, which occur in two main geographical regions: the Lower Rhône Valley (perhaps due to the influences of the Greek colony of Marseille, established in 600 BC) and central Europe. In the last two centuries BC figural imagery became more common, and bronze representations of animals, especially boars, may have had a quasi-religious function. The unique gilt-silver cult-cauldron from Gundestrup in Jutland, which probably dates to the second or first century BC, has long been accepted as important evidence for Celtic religious iconography. Its inner and outer plates are decorated with mythological scenes and deities, some of which betray exotic, eastern influences. But many features of the imagery are undoubtedly Celtic – the torc-bearing antlered god and the ram-horned serpent belong to the religious repertoire of Gaul – and the soldiers depicted bear Celtic Iron Age arms. Controversy surrounds the cauldron's place of manufacture: the best silversmiths of the period came from Thrace and Dacia in south-east Europe, and the vessel could have been made by foreign craftsmen for Celtic use. Such smiths may have heard descriptions of exotic creatures and thus included them in their art. There have been recent arguments in favour of an Indian origin for the Gundestrup Cauldron, but these conjectures overlook the close links between its religious art and that of Celtic Europe. The presence of the vessel in Denmark may be the result of looting by the Teutonic Cimbri from Gaulish territory.

Once Roman culture was established, its presence interacted on Celtic religious traditions which had previously been unexpressed in material terms. This interaction resulted in wide-scale representation of the gods, many of whom were totally alien to the Graeco-Roman pantheon. It also produced the tradition of dedicatory inscriptions which has given us names for Celtic divinities. This abundance of religious evidence, which expressed itself only under Roman influence, argues for the presence of a complex system of belief already in existence in the free Celtic period.

## Archaeology and literature

Of the three groups of evidence summarised above, only archaeology and the vernacular sources contribute substantially to the construction of Celtic myth. In essence these two strands of mythological evidence have to be treated virtually as separate entities. Because of the chronological and spatial divergences already outlined, it is not possible to perceive the two as part of the same continuum of evidence. Nonetheless it is undoubtedly true that some links can be established between the material and literary sources. There are features common to both, which are too idiosyncratic to be due to chance: the sanctity of 'three'; the symbolism of cauldrons; the supernatural power of the human head; beliefs in an Otherworld similar to earthly life are a few of the traditions which bridge the gulf between the two main strands of testimony for Celtic myth.

# The divine race of Ireland

The *Book of Invasions* records a series of successive mythical occupations of Ireland, beginning with an expedition led by Cesair and culminating in the coming of the Gaels (Celts). Indeed the function of this Myth of Invasions is to explain the presence of the historical Celts in Ireland. The central characters of the myth are the Tuatha Dé Danann (the 'People of the Goddess Danu'), a race of gods. A previous invader was Partholón who led the first colonisation of Ireland after the Flood. He came from Greece with his family and a large retinue, including three druids. Partholón and his people were wiped out by a plague. His character survives in modern Irish folklore as a fertility demon.

The last invaders chronicled in the *Book of Invasions* were the Gaels, the first Celts, speakers of a Goidelic language. According to mythic tradition the Gaels were descendants of the Sons of Míl, who came to Ireland from Spain. They dispossessed the Tuatha Dé, causing them to create a new kingdom beneath the earth. When the Gaels reached Ireland, they encountered three eponymous goddesses of the land, Banbha, Fódla and Ériu. Each demanded a promise from the invaders that, if they were successful in establishing themselves in Ireland, they would name the land after her. The seer or *fili* (see page 66) Amhairghin assured Ériu that Ireland would bear her name and, in return, Ériu prophesied that the land would belong to the Gaels for all time.

## The Tuatha Dé Danann

This race of divine beings, the mythical inhabitants of Ireland before the Celts, traced their beginnings back to their goddess-ancestress Danu. They brought with them to Ireland four powerful talismans: the Stone of Fál, which cried out at the touch of the rightful king; the Spear of Lugh, which guaranteed victory; the Sword of Nuadu, from which none escaped; and the Cauldron of the Daghda, from which no one departed unsatisfied. The Tuatha Dé were skilled in magic and in druid lore. Many of the gods were associated with particular functions: thus Oghma was skilled in war-craft; Lugh in arts and crafts; Goibhniu in smithing; Dian Cécht in medicine.

The most prominent gods of the Tuatha Dé Danann had special myths and stories associated with them and their skills. The Daghda (the 'Good God') was the tribal father-god, provider of plenty and regeneration. His two main attributes were a great club, of which one end killed and the other restored to

*Small bronze horse-head mask, from Stanwick, Yorkshire, from the first century AD. It may have been a chariot-fitting. The artist has captured the spirit of the horse in a few simple lines.*

life, and an enormous, inexhaustible cauldron. The image of the Daghda contains paradox: he is portrayed as gross and uncouth, a ridiculous, grotesque figure, who wears an indecently short tunic and eats an outrageous amount, while at the same time he is a powerful father of his tribe. This, though, is all part of his symbolism as god of fertility. Various legends concern his union with different goddesses, including Boann, goddess of the River Boyne. His coupling with the fearsome battle-fury, the Morrigán, ensures security for his people.

Goibhniu was one of a triad of craft-gods: he was the smith, Luchta the wright and Creidhne the metalworker. Together they forged magical weapons (each made a different part) for Lugh and the Tuatha Dé in their great battle against the Fomorians, local demons who pitted themselves against all invaders of Ireland. Goibhniu is the most developed character of the triad. His weapons always flew true and always killed. He had an additional role as host of the Otherworld Feast, where his special ale gave immortality. Dian Cécht, god of the craft of healing, derived his power from a combination of magic and herb-lore; he was at the same time a doctor and a smith. Thus he made the king Nuadu a silver arm to replace that which he lost in battle. Dian Cécht had the power to heal by magic: he restored dead members of the Tuatha Dé Danann by chanting incantations over a well in which the slain warriors were immersed. Manannán was a sea-god, and he is surrounded by marine imagery: his cloak was like the sea and the waves were his horses. He was also a magician (like his Welsh cognate Manawydan) and he provided help for the Tuatha Dé in their battles, including a boat which obeyed the thoughts of its sailor; a horse which travelled equally happily on sea and land; and a sword, Fragarach ('Answerer'), which could penetrate any armour. Manannán's magic pigs were symbols of regeneration: they could be killed and eaten one day and alive again the next, ready to be slaughtered for feasting.

Two of the best-known gods of the Tuatha Dé Danann are Nuadu and Lugh. Nuadu was king of the Tuatha Dé, but he had to relinquish his power after he lost his arm in battle: Insular rulers had to be physically perfect. During the interregnum, when Nuadu was temporarily disqualified from his leadership, a surrogate king was appointed. This was Bres ('the Beautiful'), a curious choice since he was half-Fomorian. His reign was not good: his niggardly ways caused Ireland's prosperity to fail. After the defeat of the Fomorians by the Tuatha Dé Danann, Bres was spared in return for his agreement to advise the Tuatha Dé on agricultural matters. Interestingly the Tuatha Dé were good at war and crafts but had no farming skills: for these they had to rely on the indigenous Fomorians. Nuadu was restored to the kingship after Dian Cécht made him a new arm, and he was thereafter known as Nuadu Argatlámh ('Nuadu of the Silver Arm'). But Nuadu was demoralised by the constant conflict with the Fomorians, and the young Lugh took over as leader. Nuadu may be identified with Nodens, the healer-god of Lydney in Gloucestershire: both names may mean 'Cloud-Maker', as if perhaps they were weather-gods.

Lugh ('Shining One') was related by blood both to the Tuatha Dé Danann and the Fomorians. He was a god of light, whose summer festival was Lughnasad. The Gaulish word *lugos* can mean 'raven', and there is a tenuous link between Lugh and these birds. Lugh was a warrior-hero, a sorcerer and master of crafts. He presented himself thus at the royal court of Nuadu at Tara. The association between Lugh and crafts has led some scholars to identify him with the Gaulish Mercury, whom Caesar describes as 'inventor of all the arts'. It was Lugh who exhorted Nuadu to stand up to the Fomorians, and he orchestrated the military campaigns which led to their rout. He himself slew the formidable Balor, leader of the Fomorians (and Lugh's own grandfather). In battle Lugh used both his own magic and the enchanted sword and boat of Manannán. Lugh's 'surname' was Lámfhada ('of the Long Arm'), a possible reflection of his skill with the throwing-spear or the sling (with which weapon he killed Balor).

The myths of Lugh are not confined to the *Book of Invasions*. In the Ulster Cycle the god appears as the Otherworld father of Cú Chulainn, who soothes and heals the young hero after his confrontations with the forces of Connacht.

After the dispossession of the Tuatha Dé Danann by the Gaels, the defeated gods establish a realm beneath the earth, a mirror-image of the upper world. Even though they are vanquished, they are able to deprive the Gaels of corn and milk, and they use this power to drive a bargain with them. So it is by mutual agreement that Ireland is divided into two parts, an upper and lower world. In their underworld kingdom the Tuatha Dé continue to control the supernatural by means of their magic. Each god possesses a *sídh* (a fairy mound), which is part of the Happy Otherworld.

## The battles for Ireland: the Fir Bholg and the Fomorians

In establishing themselves as lords of Ireland, the Tuatha Dé Danann had to fight two formidable groups of beings, each of whom was instrumental in shaping the 'history' of the island. The previous invaders, ousted by the Tuatha Dé, were the Fir Bholg, a mythical pre-Celtic people who probably took their name from a god, Builg. The Tuatha Dé defeated the Fir Bholg at the First Battle of Magh Tuiredh, and drove them into exile on the Aran Islands, where they are credited with building the massive fort of Dun Aonghusa on Inishmore. According to one tradition the Tuatha Dé allowed the Fir Bholg to retain the province of Connacht. It was at Magh Tuiredh that Nuadu lost his arm.

The second group the Tuatha Dé Danann had to face were the Fomorians or Fomhoire ('Under-demons'), a race of demonic beings who were permanent residents of Ireland, whom Partholón had already encountered in his earlier invasion and whom he fought in Ireland's first battle. When the Tuatha Dé occupied the land, the Fomorians caused them great trouble, pillaging their territory and imposing crippling taxes, with dreadful punishments for defaulters. The Fomorians had an awesome leader, Balor of the Baleful Eye, the gaze of whose single great eye caused instant death, and who could not be slain by any weapon. Balor dwelt on Tory Island, in constant dread of the fulfilment of a prophecy, namely his eventual destruction by his grandson. Despite his attempts to forestall this end (by keeping his daughter Eithne away from men) she became pregnant and gave birth to triplets. Balor cast them into the sea, but one survived: this was Lugh, who grew up to lead the Tuatha Dé against the Fomorians and who himself killed Balor with a slingshot through his eye.

The Fomorians are a divine race, like the Tuatha Dé Danann themselves. Balor represents the negative forces of evil whose power can only be neutralised by the light-force of Lugh, himself half-Fomorian and a relative of Balor. The Tuatha Dé and the Fomorians may represent the archetypal dualism between light and the chthonic (earthbound or underworld) forces, involving conflict but also mutual dependence. This last is demonstrated both by the ancestry of Lugh and by the Fomorians' agricultural skills which were necessary to the well-being of the Tuatha Dé Danann.

## Sacral kingship

A powerful concept which underpins much of Insular myth is that of the sacral or divine king. The ruler of Ireland was inextricably linked to the fortunes and prosperity of the land itself. Thus the niggardliness of King Bres led to a blight of barrenness upon Ireland. The royal court of Tara was traditionally the sacred site of royal inauguration; here the ritual marriage was enacted between the king and the land, personified as the goddess of sovereignty. Ériu was one such personification, an eponymous goddess of Ireland who offered a golden goblet of red wine to successive mortal kings as a symbol of their union and of the florescence of the land. Medb of Connacht cohabited with nine kings, and no man could rule in Tara unless he first mated with her. A symbol of this union of divinity with mortal is the transformation of the goddess, often from an old hag to a young girl of great beauty.

The king-elect had to undergo various tests to prove the validity of his claim: the royal mantle had to fit him; the royal chariot must accept him; the Stone of Fál at Tara must shriek when touched by him. The rightful king must

*This stone relief comes from a healing shrine at Mavilly, France, and is Romano-Celtic. It depicts a Celtic version of Mars, a protector against disease, with a goddess and ram-horned snake, symbol of regeneration and fertility.*

*Bronze stag, first century BC, from a religious hoard at Neuvy-en-Sullias, France.*

19

be seen in a dream by the participant at the *tarbhfhess* or bull-sleep. Once elected, the king was hedged about with *geissi*, bonds or sacred rules of conduct, the betrayal of which would cause his downfall.

## The Fionn Cycle

The Fionn Cycle belongs, in its developed form, to the twelfth century, although it contains earlier elements. Its central character is the supernatural hero Finn mac Cumhaill (sometimes written as Finn macCool). He is the leader of the Fianna, an élite war-band whose members are chosen by rigorous ordeals of strength and valour and whose conduct is controlled by strict rules and codes. The Fianna are pledged to support the king of Ireland against any invaders.

The divine status of Finn is demonstrated by many features of his life. He is reared by a druidess and he very early develops a strong affinity with the natural world symbolised, indeed, by his marriage to Sava, an enchanted woman, transformed to a deer by the evil force of the Black Druid. Finn's attainment of manhood is surrounded by mythological events: he acquires wisdom from Finnegas the Bard by eating the Salmon of Knowledge, for whom Finnegas has fished for seven years. When Finn arrives at Tara, his first act is to use magic to rid the court of Aillen, a malicious goblin who sets fire to the palace every year at the Celtic festival of Samhain (31 October/1 November). Throughout his life Finn has encounters with the supernatural world, hunting enchanted animals who entice him to the Otherworld, and meeting divinities such as the Morrigán, Nuadu and Oenghus. He has the gift of prophecy and is endowed with superhuman battle-prowess. Finn's death is linked with a *geis* or bond that he must never drink from a horn. When the ageing hero is abandoned by the Fianna, he tries to prove his strength by leaping the Boyne, but he has broken his *geis* and perishes in the river.

In the Fionn Cycle, Finn is linked to other supernatural beings and happenings. His association with the young Diarmaid, his rival for the beautiful Gráinne's affection, shows him in a less than favourable light. His jealousy causes him to bring about Diarmaid's death by magic (see page 39). This episode illustrates a typical aspect of Insular myth, the triangle of young lover, girl and ageing suitor, a theme with a precise parallel in the Ulster tale of Conchobar, Deirdre and Naoise (see pages 39–40).

Finn's son Oisin ('Little Deer') is strongly associated with the Otherworld. He is bewitched by Niav of the Golden Hair, daughter of the king of Tir na n' Og the ('Land of Forever Young'), and he goes to live with her. But he is homesick and plans to visit the upper world, against Niav's advice. She warns him never to set foot on Irish soil if he wishes to return to her. Oisin makes the journey, only to find that 300 years have passed. As he realises this, his harness breaks, he falls from his horse and, as he strikes the ground, dies instantly of extreme old age.

# Myths of the Ulster Cycle

The group of epic prose tales known collectively as the Ulster Cycle concerns the activities of the Ulaid or Ulstermen, particularly their great conflict with the neighbouring province of Connacht, and the exploits of their hero, Cú Chulainn. Central to the cycle is the *Táin Bó Cuailnge*, or *Cattle Raid of Cooley*, probably first composed in the eighth century AD. The *Táin* is preserved in a number of major versions of which the earliest is in the *Leabhar na h Uidre* (the *Book of the Dun Cow*), compiled at Clonmacnois, Co. Offaly, by three monks, one of whom died in 1106. While it has generally been assumed that the Ulster Cycle was a late compilation of a much earlier oral tradition, scholars have recently put forward convincing arguments for its original composition as literature which was orally transmitted during the early historical period.

The considerable mythological content of the Ulster Cycle is very evident. Although compiled within a Christian milieu, the early monastic scribes may well have been the *filidh*, the keepers of past knowledge, who were steeped in the ancient ritual traditions and whose purpose it was to preserve myth in written form (See 'Druids, sacrifice and ritual', page 66). There is no problem about the acceptance of some continuity of religious and ritual tradition from pagan Ireland into the Christian period.

## The *Táin Bó Cuailnge* (*Cattle Raid of Cooley*)

The dominance of mythology in the Ulster Cycle is demonstrated dramatically by its central theme, the *Táin*, which describes the great war between Ulster and Connacht over a huge bull, the Donn ('Brown') of Cuailnge in Ulster. The story is not about cattle-rustling as a normal secular pastime, but about one fantastic and supernatural animal, around whom was woven a great quest- and battle-myth. The story begins with a foretale in which Queen Medb and her consort Ailill of Connacht boast, while in bed one night, of their respective possessions. The pair are fairly evenly matched save for one thing: Ailill owns a great white-horned bull, the Findbennach. Medb searches her land in vain for a creature of comparable splendour, but she learns of the great Brown Bull of Ulster, owned by one Daire mac Fiachniu, who agrees to lend the Donn to the queen in return for a large reward. However, on overhearing a brag made by Medb's men, to the effect that they would have taken the bull with or without his owner's consent, Daire refuses Medb and sends the Donn into hiding. Medb

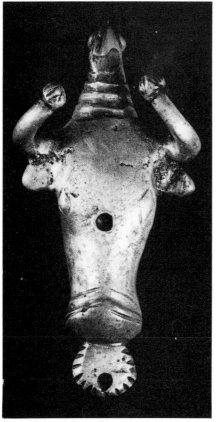

*Front and side views of a bronze bucket-escutcheon in the form of a bull's head surmounted by that of an eagle, from Thealby, Lincolnshire. Late Iron Age.*

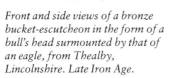

*Small bronze statuette of Mars with ram-horned snakes. It comes from a hoard of figurines found at Southbroom, Wiltshire and is Romano-Celtic.*

decides to invade Ulster and seize the Donn by force, and there ensues a long-drawn-out war between the two provinces. On the night before the final confrontation, the Donn is sent into Connacht for safety. He bellows loudly at the scent of new territory and Ailill's Findbennach hears the intruder: no one but he before now has dared to make such a noise in his domain. Queen Medb's men appoint the mischief-maker Bricriu (a divine figure) as judge in the fight between the two bulls. The animals battle all day and night, all over Ireland. The Donn of Cuailnge eventually prevails, impaling Ailill's Findbennach on his horns, but he does not survive the conflict and dies of exhaustion.

The combat of the bulls symbolises the struggle between Ulster and Connacht: their death signals peace following the Pyrrhic victory of the Ulstermen. It is quite clear from the *Táin* that both bulls are of supernatural origin. Each is famed for his size and strength. The Donn is so big that fifty boys can ride on his back at once. The hero Ferghus comments that the two animals were sent purposely to Ireland by jealous gods, in order to cause war and bitterness among the people. He describes how the bulls are enchanted, metamorphosed creatures, who were originally swineherds and then took a succession of different forms, but had always been a source of strife and destruction. The Brown Bull is capable of human understanding: he responds immediately when Cormac exhorts him to ever greater efforts against the great bull of Connacht.

## Cú Chulainn and other Ulster heroes

Three warriors stand out among the mythical heroes of Ulster: Ferghus mac Roich, Conall Cernach and – greatest champion of all – Cú Chulainn. The descriptions of all three betray their superhuman, semi-divine status. The first part of Ferghus' name is cognate with the Latin *vir* (man) and he is associated with fertility imagery: he is the first lover of Queen Medb, herself notoriously promiscuous, and mate of the nature-goddess Flidais. Ferghus is described as having a rampaging sexual appetite, requiring seven women to satisfy it. His image is that of a supernatural figure; he has the strength of 700 men; he is as tall as a giant; and at one meal he can consume seven pigs, seven deer, seven cows and seven vats of liquor. He possesses a magic sword, long as a rainbow.

Ferghus belongs to the court of King Conchobar of Ulster, and is foster-father to the young Cú Chulainn, but a particular episode causes the defection of himself and other heroes to Medb's court. This is the elopement of the lovers Deirdre and Naoise, and Conchobar's treachery (see page 40). Some scholars are of the opinion that the Deirdre episode was added to the *Táin* specifically to explain Ferghus' defection. Once at Connacht, Ferghus liaises between Medb and Cú Chulainn. He dies at the hands of Ailill, while bathing in a pool with Medb. Some traditions credit Ferghus with authorship of the *Táin*.

Conall Cernach is the son of Amhairghin the poet and Fionnchaomh, daughter of the druid Cathbadh. 'Conall' means 'strong as a wolf'; 'Cernach' means 'victorious'. Like Ferghus, Conall has a large element of the supernatural in his imagery: he is the guardian of Ireland's boundaries and is clearly an ancestor-deity of part of the land. Again like Ferghus, he is a foster-father and tutor to Cú Chulainn. Conall is the epitome of the Irish champion: at the Feast of Bricriu (an Otherworld banquet), he boasts that he always sleeps with the severed head of a Connachtman beneath his knee. In the essentially similar tale of Mac Da Thó's Pig, he is described as wearing the head of Connacht's best warrior at his belt. Conall's status as semi-divine hero is attested by many episodes in his life; one tale relates his attack on a fort whose treasure is guarded by a great serpent. An affinity between hero and snake is displayed when the creature dives into Conall's waist-band and neither harms the other.

Cú Chulainn (the 'Hound of Culann') is the archetypal superhuman champion of epic tradition: 'Cú' is a common title for a warrior, but in this case the hound epithet has a specific meaning which relates to an episode in Cú Chulainn's childhood. When very young, he kills the hound of Culann the Smith, and pledges himself to guard the smithy in the dog's place. This dog-association continues throughout Cú Chulainn's life: he has a *geis* or bond on him not to partake of dog-flesh; he breaks the bond and thus sets the scene for his own destruction.

Cú Chulainn is destined to have a short but glorious life. He is brave, beautiful, strong, an invincible warrior. His identity may indeed derive from a warrior-cult, whence he was euhemerised into a pseudo-historical figure. His conception, life and death are closely linked with the supernatural. His father may have been the god Lugh or Conchobar, and there is incest (a mark of divinity) in his immediate ancestry. As occurs with the Welsh Pryderi, Cú Chulainn's birth is interlocked with that of horses: two foals are born at exactly the same moment as the hero, and they become his chariot-horses, the Grey of Macha and the Black of Saingliu. Cú Chulainn himself displays superhuman status from boyhood: he arrives at Conchobar's court of Emhain Macha, having routed 150 of the king's youth brigade. While still a boy, he demands arms, having heard a prophecy that whoever took up arms on a certain day should have a glorious future. Cú Chulainn breaks fifteen sets of weapons before he accepts the specially strengthened arms of Conchobar himself.

The young warrior is trained by Scáthach, a female teacher of warcraft and prophetess, who foretells Cú Chulainn's future through divination. He goes to war bearing magical weapons and armour, including the Gae Bulga, a barbed spear which inflicts only fatal wounds, and a visor, gift of Manannán the sea-god. Cú Chulainn's charioteer has the power to cast a spell of invisibility over his chariot. Cú Chulainn is the main champion of Ulster against the forces of Connacht, and of all the Ulstermen only he is exempt from Macha's curse, a weakness inflicted upon them in time of crisis. He kills huge numbers of Medb's forces single-handed. When the battle-rage is on him, he goes into 'warp-spasm', a berserk fit when he can no longer distinguish friend from foe. When berserk, he becomes a monster: his body spins within its skin; his hair stands on end, surrounded by a halo of light; his muscles swell; one eye bulges, the other sinks into his head; his howl causes all the local spirits to howl with him, driving the enemy mad with terror.

*Bronze sculpture by Oliver Shepherd, 1916, now in the main Post Office, Dublin. It shows the death of Cú Chulainn, the raven-goddess Morrigán or Badbh perched on his shoulder to signify that he is dead and safe to approach. The Ulster hero bound himself to a tree in order to stay standing even in death.*

The supernatural symbolism surrounding Cú Chulainn is intense: he uses magic to halt the advance of the Connachtmen; he has magical power over animals; he is linked with sacred numbers, having triple-coloured hair, seven pupils in each eye and seven digits on each hand and foot. He is closely associated with the divine: his foster-father (or natural father) is Lugh; he has many encounters with the war-goddess, the Morrigán; and he visits the Otherworld while still alive. Cú Chulainn is present at the Feast of Bricriu, a divine mischief-maker who foments strife and rivalry between warriors. At the feast Bricriu causes jealousy between the heroes Cú Chulainn, Conall Cernach and Loeghaire by offering each the champion's portion of pork.

Cú Chulainn's death at Magh Muirtheimne is surrounded with portents: when harnessed for the final battle, the Grey of Macha weeps tears of blood, and when Cú Chulainn mounts his chariot, all his weapons fall at his feet. Lastly he encounters the 'Washer at the Ford' washing his armour, a sure sign of doom in Insular myth. Cú Chulainn dies fighting, killed with a spear forged by Vulcan. The hero-light around his head dims and his death is signalled by the Badbh or the Morrigán, divine destroyers who, in raven-form, perch on his shoulder, emboldening the Connachtmen to come forward and decapitate him.

This is a chant of Cú Chulainn in his great conflict with Medb, referring to the mediator Ferghus:

My skill in arms grows great
On fine armies cowering
I let fall famous blows
On whole hosts I wage war
To crush their chief hero
and Medb and Ailill also
Who stir up wrong, red hatred

And black woman-wailing,
Who march in cruel treachery
Trampling their chief hero
And his sage, sound advice
– a fierce, right-speaking warrior
Full of noble acts.
(trans. Kinsella, 1969)

## Medb and Conchobar

The opposed provinces of Ulster and Connacht are respectively ruled by Conchobar and Medb. Conchobar mac Nessa is a mythical king of Ulster, who rules from the royal court of Emhain Macha (which has been identified with Navan Fort near Armagh). Excavations have shown that the main occupation period, around 700 BC, focused on a large circular timber building standing beside a larger enclosure. In about 100 BC this 'royal' residence was replaced by a ceremonial building or sanctuary, a huge structure consisting of five circles of oak posts with, in the centre, a massive oak pillar which could be seen for miles.

Conchobar is very closely linked with war: he has a war-band known as the Red Branch Knights, of whom Cú Chulainn becomes chief. In addition Conchobar raises a youth-corps, trained as young boys in war-craft. The Ulster king's rule is steeped in myth and the supernatural. That he is a sacral king, appointed by druids, is demonstrated by an episode in the war with Connacht: when the defector Ferghus strikes the king's shield, it shrieks, as always happens when a sacred Irish ruler is in danger. Conchobar himself has prophetic powers, but most prophecy is in the hands of the royal druid Cathbadh, who repeatedly foretells the future of Ulster. He prophesies the doom to be caused by the beauty of Deirdre (see page 40); the glorious life of Cú Chulainn; and he warns the Ulstermen against the destructive satire of the poet Aithirne. One of Cathbadh's responsibilities is to instruct young heroes in the craft of divination, the plotting of which days were lucky or unlucky for specific events or activities.

Conchobar is a complex character. He is related to Cú Chulainn as either foster-father, grandfather or natural father, and was once married to Medb before she became ruler of Connacht. His honour-code, unlike that of the archetypal hero, is flawed and his treachery to Naoise and cruelty to Deirdre bring about the defection of three prominent Ulster warriors. Conchobar meets his death by means of a brainball made from the head of the Leinster king Meas Geaghra (a brainball was made by mixing human brains with lime and allowing the mixture to harden). This curious but effective weapon was hurled at the Ulster king by Ceat mac Mághach in revenge for a wrong.

Medb ('She Who Intoxicates') is queen of Connacht, ruling variously at Tara and Cruachain, but in reality she is a euhemerised deity. Medb is a goddess of sovereignty and, in addition, she may be perceived as one of the group of Insular goddesses of war, sexuality and territory. Her rampant promiscuity symbolises Ireland's fertility, and the association of her name with alcoholic drink (specifically mead) is linked with the concept of the union between sovereignty goddess and mortal ruler, which is sanctified by the offering of a cup of liquor by the goddess to the king. Other demonstrations of Medb's divine status include her ability to change shape from hag to young girl, a characteristic of the Insular goddesses. She also shares with these deities the ability to wreak destruction: she brings about the deaths of Ferghus, Conall Cernach, her husband Ailill and Cú Chulainn. Medb's presence, driving round the battlefield in her chariot, can unman warriors; she can run with superhuman speed, and she has animal-familiars, a bird and a squirrel.

The great war between Ulster and Connacht is brought about largely by Medb's jealousy of Ailill, whose great bull she covets. She is warned by her poet and prophetess Fedelma that her enemy Cú Chulainn will destroy most of her army. Medb pits her wits against the Ulster champion, tries to bribe him with her daughter Finnebair and finally uses magic to bring about his death. Her own demise, chronicled in an eleventh-century text, occurs as a revenge-killing. She is slain by her nephew Furbaidhe whose mother, Clothra, Medb has murdered. The great queen-goddess meets an ignominious end, killed by a slingshot made of a lump of hard cheese.

## The battle-furies

Three goddesses occur repeatedly in the Ulster Cycle: Macha, the Badbh and the Morrigán. They share the characteristic of possessing both single and triple form. In addition they all have a close link with animals: Macha has an affinity with horses; and like the Badbh and the Morrigán she has the ability to metamorphose from human form to that of a crow or raven. Each goddess is concerned with warfare and is, at the same time, a symbol of promiscuous sexuality.

*Romano-Celtic bronze bull, triple-horned, from Glanum, southern France.*

27

Macha is perceived as both one and three entities, but each of these three possesses a partially separate identity. One Macha, wife of Nemedh, a leader of the third mythical invasion of Ireland, is a prophetess who foresees the destruction of the country wrought by the *Táin* conflict. The second Macha is a warrior-ruler of Ireland. In her third identity Macha is a divine bride, the wife of a human, Crunnchu. Because Macha is a swift runner, her husband brags that she can outrun the king's horses. He has to make good his boast and, although Macha is about to give birth, she is forced to compete. She wins the race but dies giving birth to twins and with her dying breath curses the men of Ulster: at moments of crisis they will fall victim to a weakness as severe as that of a woman in childbirth, for five days and four nights.

Macha gave her name to the royal Ulster court of Emhain Macha ('Macha's Twins'). Her equine association is shown not only by her speed but also by the name of Cú Chulainn's horse, the Grey of Macha. She is a complex deity: prophet, warrior, ruler and goddess of sovereignty and fertility, closely bound up with the fortunes of the land itself.

The Badbh is essentially a goddess of battle and its destructive qualities. Her name evokes images of violence, fury and war. Like the Morrigán she may appear as woman or crow: one of her names is Badbh Catha ('Battle-Crow'). She is both a single and a triple goddess. Her power on the battlefield is psychological: her presence confounds and terrifies soldiers and she wreaks havoc, particularly among the Connachtmen. Badbh is a prophetess of doom and death. She helps Cú Chulainn, but alights in bird-form on his shoulder when he dies. She appears as a 'Washer at the Ford', rinsing the arms of a warrior who will shortly die in battle. In the story of Da Derga's Hostel, she appears to the doomed king Conaire as three black, crow-like hags: the imagery of bird and woman is merged.

The Morrigán ('Phantom Queen') strongly resembles the Badbh. She is particularly linked to Cú Chulainn: on one occasion, she appears to him as a beautiful girl but he, impatient for battle, brusquely spurns her advances. In revenge the Morrigán attacks him, changing form rapidly from eel to wolf to red heifer. Cú Chulainn wins but is exhausted. The Morrigán now appears to the hero in the form of an old woman milking a cow: she offers him milk and, in return, he blesses her, healing her wounds. Like the Badbh the Morrigán's most frequent appearance is as a death-crow, prophesying death on the battlefield. In this form she warns the Donn of Cuailnge that he will die. As a war-fury she unnerves armies and she, too, is a 'Washer at the Ford', a harbinger of death. But her prophecies are not always doom-laden: one episode in the 'Mythological Cycle' concerns her advice to the Daghda on how to deal with the Fomorians, enemies of the Tuatha Dé Danann.

In addition to her war-death role the Morrigán has powerful sexual imagery. This is seen most clearly in her mating with the tribal god, the Daghda, while astride a river. She is recalled in an Irish place-name, 'The Paps of the Morrigán'. She is a fertility-goddess, and her coupling with the god of the tribe reflects her function as a deity of sovereignty, identified with the land of Ireland.

# Some early Welsh myths

E arly Welsh mythology survives in recognisable form only in the *Four Branches of the Mabinogi*, the *Tale of Culhwch and Olwen* and the *Dream of Rhonabwy*, together with a few fragments, such as the poem *The Spoils of Annwn*, which has been ascribed to Taliesin.

The stories contained in these earliest vernacular Welsh compilations possess consistent supernatural elements involving god-like heroes, enchanted animals and magical happenings. Sometimes it is possible to perceive a deeper or more profound cosmogony buried within the stories, myths of creation or supernatural explanations of natural phenomena.

## Pwyll, Arawn, Rhiannon and Pryderi

The First Branch of the *Mabinogi* contains the story of Pwyll, lord of Llys Arberth (Narberth), his wife Rhiannon, their son Pryderi, and the encounter between Pwyll and Arawn, lord of Annwn, the Welsh Otherworld. The meeting of Pwyll and Arawn is the first episode. It takes place when Pwyll is hunting deer and breaks his honour-code by taking another hunter's kill as his own. The hounds of this rival hunter are strange creatures, shining white with red ears (their colouring marking them as Otherworld beings – the same colours recur elsewhere in Welsh and Irish myth). The wronged huntsman is Arawn. Pwyll can redeem himself only by changing places with Arawn for a year, at the end of which he must meet, fight and kill Hafgan, Arawn's Otherworld enemy, and then return to meet Arawn at the present meeting-place, Glyn Cuch. Arawn warns Pwyll to strike Hafgan only once; if twice wounded, he will recover and be stronger than ever. An important element in the story is that both Pwyll and Arawn practise chastity in each other's households: neither ruler makes love to the wife of the other. Pwyll keeps his pledge and his year-end tryst, and thereafter the two rulers, returning to their own domains, maintain a close friendship. After Pwyll's death this relationship is preserved by his son Pryderi, to whom Arawn makes a precious gift of the first pigs in Wales. After his sojourn in Annwn, Pwyll himself is known as 'Lord of the Otherworld', a clear indication of his divine status.

This Otherworld episode is important in that it introduces a number of recurrent features of vernacular myth: the ability of certain humans to penetrate the Underworld while still alive; the need for Otherworld beings to employ full-blooded mortals to undertake certain tasks on their behalf; the use of

*The horse-goddess Epona carrying fruit, on a Romano-Celtic relief from Kastel, Germany. Epona was not only a horse-deity but also had a role as a provider of plenty.*

animals to facilitate encounters between the mundane and supernatural worlds.

The second significant episode in the First Branch, which is redolent with symbolism, concerns Pwyll and Rhiannon. While at Gorsedd Arberth (a magical meeting-place for the court), Pwyll sees a beautiful young woman in dazzling gold riding a large, shining-white horse and is strongly attracted to her. But although the horse is moving quite slowly, neither Pwyll nor his swiftest horsemen can catch up with it. In desperation Pwyll calls to the woman who immediately halts and speaks to him, introducing herself as Rhiannon and informing him that she has come to marry him in preference to her suitor, Gwawl. Pwyll wins Rhiannon by trickery (an act which has repercussions later in the *Mabinogi*); they marry and produce a son, Pryderi.

The character of Rhiannon herself is interesting in terms of myth. Her name may derive from that of a pagan goddess Rigantona ('Great – or Sacred – Queen'). The manner of her meeting with Pwyll has supernatural undertones, as does her consistent link with horses. After her alleged murder of her baby son (see below), it is Rhiannon's penance to sit beside the horse-block outside the gates of the court for seven years, offering to carry visitors up to the palace on her back, like a beast of burden. Rhiannon conforms to two archetypes of myth: in her generosity to the nobles of Llys Arberth when Pwyll brings her to court, which earns her the image of a gracious, bountiful queen-goddess; and as the 'wronged wife', falsely accused of killing her son. Rhiannon's horse-imagery and her bounty have led scholars to equate her with the Celtic horse-goddess Epona (see page 59).

Pryderi's birth is surrounded with supernatural mystery. When three nights old, he is stolen while his watch-women are asleep, and Rhiannon is wrongly blamed for his murder. The scene now shifts from Llys Arberth to the household of Teyrnon Twryf Liant, Lord of Gwent Is-Coed. Puzzling events take place here each May-eve, when Teyrnon's mare produces a foal which immediately disappears. At the same time that the boy Pryderi vanishes from Llys Arberth, Teyrnon keeps watch in the stable as his mare gives birth to her finest foal. Teyrnon sees a huge claw seize the foal, dragging it through the window. He hacks off the arm with his sword and saves his foal but, as he does so, he hears a scream and a commotion outside and runs out to investigate. It is too dark to see anything and he returns to the stable to find a baby boy lying on the threshold, wrapped in a silk shawl, a garment which signifies his noble rank.

Teyrnon and his wife foster the child, who grows with incredible speed and is far in advance of his age. At three years old the boy is given the foal. When he is four, his foster-parents note his uncanny resemblance to Pwyll and, knowing the story of the missing prince, realise that their boy must be Pryderi. He is restored to Pwyll and Rhiannon amid great rejoicing. The story of Pryderi contains considerable elements of myth: he disappears on the eve of 1 May, the great spring festival of Beltene (see page 55); and his earliest life is closely associated with that of the foal, which is also taken on May-eve. (This affinity with horses is linked with that of his mother.) Finally the kidnapping of Pryderi when three nights old is precisely similar to the fate of the young Mabon, the Welsh hunter-god of *Culhwch and Olwen*, which is discussed later in this chapter. Celtic conception tales such as this, surrounded by curious events, may be symbolic of the transcendental meaning of birth – a child born of earthly parents but also the incarnation of supernatural essence – expressed by myth. (Similar mystery, of course, surrounds the birth of Christ.) It is clear that Pwyll, Rhiannon and Pryderi all possess elements of divinity, even though their status is never precisely defined.

## Branwen and Bendigeidfran

The family ap Llyr of Harlech is the focus of the Second and Third branches of the *Mabinogi*. Their divine status is implied by their patronym 'Son of the Sea', which is cognate with the Irish god Lir. The central characters of the Second Branch are Branwen and her brother Bendigeidfran ('Brân the Blessed'), the word *brân* meaning a raven or crow. Although the Branch is named after Branwen, and therein she is described as one of the three chief ladies of the land, it is Brân whose superhuman stature dominates the story.

The tale begins with the betrothal of Branwen to Matholwch, king of Ireland. Branwen's brother Efnisien objects to the match and insults Matholwch by mutilating his horses as they stand stabled at the Harlech court. Matholwch is seemingly appeased by Bendigeidfran's gifts, greatest of which is a magical cauldron of Irish make, which can restore dead warriors to life. Matholwch and Branwen sail for Ireland, but the king's resentment smoulders and he treats his queen as a serf, sentencing her to work in the kitchens, her ears boxed each day by the butcher. Matholwch ensures that no word of this persecution can reach Wales, but Branwen herself takes a hand in her own destiny, training a starling to take word to her brother. Once Bendigeidfran hears of his sister's plight, he mobilises his army and makes war on Ireland.

Bendigeidfran, described as so large that no house can contain him, simply wades across the Irish Sea. Battle is joined and the forces of Wales win. But it is a Pyrrhic victory, and Bendigeidfran is mortally wounded by a poisoned spear. His supernatural status is displayed by his command to his men that they cut off his head and bear it with them to the White Mount in London, there to bury it facing east, so that no foreigner can invade Britain. The head of Brân has magical properties: it remains alive, conversing with his men, an uncorrupted talisman until its final interment. On their way to London with the head, Brân's men linger for seven years in Harlech and then for many more in the Happy Otherworld of Gwales, where they hear the three magical singing birds of Rhiannon. Branwen herself dies of a broken heart in Wales, at Aber Alaw, lamenting that because of her two great islands are in ruin.

Once again supernatural features run as a persistent thread through the tale: Brân's size and strength; the power of the severed head; the cauldron of resurrection; and the ability of humans to enlist the aid of animals. All these are concepts which have their parallel in Irish myth and in the symbolism expressed by pagan Celtic iconography.

## Manawydan and the enchantment of Dyfed

Manawydan ap Llyr is a brother of Branwen and Brân. He is a cognate of the Irish Manannán, son of Lir, a sea-god. The marine identity of Manawydan is not developed in the Welsh myth, but the two share common features, such as the ability to conjure magic and a reputation for trickery. The Third Branch of the *Mabinogi* develops the character of Manawydan, after whom it is named. He is a magician, a trickster, a superb craftsman. Moreover, his cultivation of wheat may constitute a mythical explanation of the introduction of arable exploitation in Wales.

After Pwyll's death, Manawydan marries his widow, Rhiannon. Following a feast at Llys Arberth, the couple go up to the Gorsedd Arberth accompanied by Pryderi and Cigfa his wife. The four witness the casting of a spell over Dyfed: all settlements and inhabitants of the land vanish and the countryside itself is shrouded in a magical mist. Since nothing is left in Dyfed, the four travel to England where Manawydan and Pryderi set up as craftsmen, saddlemakers or cobblers. But wherever they go, Manawydan's skill incites the envy and malice of other artisans, who hound them out of town after town. They return to Dyfed where they survive by hunting. On one expedition Manawydan and Pryderi have a supernatural encounter with a huge boar whose coat is dazzling white, betokening his Otherworld origins. The creature lures the hounds towards a strange castle, unknown to the hunters. Despite Manawydan's prophetic warning, Pryderi follows the dogs and falls under an enchantment: in the castle he touches a beautiful golden bowl suspended from

*Bronze group of hunters with boar and stag, of the third century BC, from Balzars, Liechtenstein. The men are dressed as soldiers, and the animals have exaggerated tusks and antlers.*

the air by chains and sticks fast to it. His feet are rooted to the ground and he cannot speak. On hearing of his fate Rhiannon follows him and she also falls under the spell of the bowl.

Bereft of his dogs, Manawydan cannot hunt and instead he begins to cultivate wheat. The crops flourish but, just before harvest, two fields are destroyed by armies of mice. Manawydan lies in wait for them as they attack the third field; all escape but one pregnant mouse, slower than the rest. Manawydan now embarks on the bizarre process of hanging the mouse, refusing pleas for mercy from several passers-by. Finally his preparations are interrupted by a bishop who attempts to redeem the mouse. Manawydan refuses to yield unless certain demands are met: Pryderi and Rhiannon must be restored, and the seven cantrefs of Dyfed released from their enchantment. (A cantref was a group of 100 farmsteads.) Thus Manawydan recognises the bishop as a fellow magician. The terms are accepted: the bishop identifies himself as one Llwyd, explaining that he cast the spells in order to avenge the wrong done by Pwyll to Rhiannon's suitor Gwawl in robbing him of his bride. The mouse is Llwyd's metamorphosed wife, sent especially with her transformed women to destroy Manawydan's corn. Dyfed is restored and the mouse returned to human form: Manawydan's magic proves the stronger.

## Math, Gwydion, Lleu and Blodeuwedd

The Fourth Branch of the *Mabinogi* concerns Gwynedd and the divine dynasty of Dôn. The story of Math, Lord of Gwynedd, may represent an early narrative, which is in fact a Myth of Creation and Fall belonging to the pre-Christian Celts. This may explain the curious description of Math himself who, unless at war, has to sit with his feet in the lap of a virgin: he depends on this contact in order to remain alive, and the virginity of the foot-holder is essential.

And at that time Math son of Mathonwy would not be alive, except while his feet were in the lap of a virgin, unless it were the disturbance of war which prevented him.
(Jones and Jones, 1976)

33

The most likely interpretation for this piece of myth is that some kind of sacral kingship is represented, whereby the life-force of the land is concentrated within the virgin, with her undissipated and undiluted sexuality. There may be a parallel with the Insular tradition of a ritual marriage between mortal king and goddess of sovereignty, the personified force of the territory, in order that the land may prosper and be fertile. If Math's contact with the virgin foot-holder does similarly signify a link with the well-being of Gwynedd, the fact that war releases him from this bond may mean that warfare is perceived to generate a life-force of its own.

In 'Math' war breaks out between Gwynedd and Dyfed, fomented by Math's nephew Gwydion, who robs Pryderi of his pigs by means of magic trickery. Gwydion's brother Gilfaethwy lusts after Math's foot-holder Goewin, and while Math is at war the two brothers conspire to rob her of her virginity. Some scholars liken the rape of Goewin to the Fall from Grace of Adam and Eve, an act which heralds trouble and sorrow for humankind. When Math returns, his fury causes him to punish the brothers, turning them for three consecutive years into pairs of different animals: a stag and hind; a boar and sow; and a wolf and she-wolf. The brothers swap sexes each time and, every year, they produce animal-offspring. These children Math restores to human form but they retain their animal-names, thus maintaining their link with wild nature:

> The three sons of false Gilfaethwy,
> Three champions true,
> Bleiddwn, Hyddwn, Hychdwn.
> (trans. Jones and Jones, 1976)

The second important episode in 'Math' concerns Arianrhod and her son. Arianrhod applies to Math for the vacant post of virgin foot-holder, but she fails the test of purity, giving birth to two sons as she steps over Math's magical staff. The main story concerns the fate of the second boy, on whom his mother places three curses: one that he shall have no name unless she agrees to name him; another that he shall bear no arms unless she equips him herself; the third that he shall have no mortal wife. The magician Gwydion tricks Arianrhod into naming the boy – Lleu Llaw Gyffes (the 'Bright One of the Skilful Hand') – and into arming him. Math and Gwydion together conjure a wife for Lleu, created from the flowers of oak, broom and meadowsweet and named Blodeuwedd.

The character of Lleu is beset with enigma and paradox from the time of his birth to a mother who is apparently virgin. His destiny imposed upon him by his hostile mother is interesting: she denies him name, weapons and a wife, the three rites of passage which are necessary for the attainment of manhood. It is only by Gwydion's magic that Lleu can reach maturity. Lleu's death is equally contradictory: he cannot be killed inside or out-of-doors, neither on land nor water, neither naked nor clothed, and only by a spear made at a time when work is forbidden. Such a 'difficult' death generally involves a woman's betrayal and it is so here. Blodeuwedd, born without roots and thus without moral sense, is faithless; she and her lover Gronw Pebyr conspire to murder Lleu by causing him to reveal to his wife the secret formula by which he can be slain. When Lleu adopts the only position in which he is vulnerable, the hidden Gronw spears him but, instead of dying, Lleu screams and, turning into an eagle, flies into an oak tree. Here Gwydion finds him, enticing him down with song and restoring him to human form. In direct contrast Blodeuwedd is punished by being turned into an owl, shunned by all other birds and condemned to hunt alone at night.

Lleu is probably an ancient British god, perhaps cognate with the Irish Lugh (see page 17) with whom he shares a name associated with light. His birth, destiny and immortality imply his divine status, as does the care taken to protect him by the magician Gwydion. The deception, riddle and contradiction which underpin 'Math' are all devices common to myth and may be found equally in the Irish tradition and in stories of the Graeco-Roman pantheon.

## Culhwch, Olwen and Twrch Trwyth

In *Culhwch and Olwen* the supernatural is ever-present; there are beings who are of indisputably divine status. Mabon ('Divine Youth'), a hunter-god, is son of Modron ('Mother'), arguably a reference to a Welsh mother-goddess cult. He resembles Pryderi in that both are stolen when three nights old. The archetypal 'Young Man' represented by Mabon has its Irish parallel in Oenghus. It is in *Culhwch and Olwen* that Gofannon, the smith-god, appears; he is cognate with the Irish Goibnhiu (see page 16), the divine smith of the Tuatha Dé Danann.

Culhwch is of royal blood, the cousin of Arthur. Both Culhwch's birth and his name betray an affinity with animals: before he is born his mother develops a violent antipathy to pigs and, on passing a herd, gives birth in her fright and then flees, abandoning the baby. The child is found by the swineherd who names him Culhwch ('Pig-run') and restores him to his parents Cilydd and Goleuddyd. The link between Culhwch's birth and pigs betrays supernatural influence similar to that of Pryderi and the foal (see pages 30–31).

Goleuddyd dies and Cilydd remarries: the new wife has a daughter whom she wishes Culhwch to wed, but he demurs on the grounds of his youth. The queen curses the boy, proclaiming that the only woman Culhwch will ever marry is Olwen, daughter of Ysbaddaden, Chief Giant. On hearing Olwen's name, Culhwch falls passionately in love with her and pledges himself to find her. Cilydd suggests that Culhwch go to visit Arthur, ostensibly to get his hair cut: this presumably represents a rite of passage from youth to manhood. Culhwch sets out in splendour, like a young god or hero, with a glowing aura about his face, fully armed with a battle-axe, a golden sword and a hatchet which 'can make the air bleed'. He has an ivory hunting-horn and two grey-hounds and is mounted on a great horse. As Culhwch reaches Arthur's court, his superhuman, godlike rank is revealed: the keeper of the gate refuses the unan-nounced Culhwch entry; the hero responds by threatening to utter three shouts that will make women barren and cause those who are pregnant to abort. The threat of barrenness probably symbolises Culhwch's ability to make Arthur's crops and herds infertile as well.

*Bronze boar of the late first century BC or early first century AD, found in the Lexden Tumulus, a British chieftain's grave, at Colchester. The animal has an erect dorsal crest, symbolic of aggression and ferocity.*

Culhwch persuades Arthur to help him in his search for Olwen, and the story now reveals itself as a Quest Tale. After a year Olwen is found and told of Culhwch's love. Her appearance and the heavy gold torc that she wears indicate her high rank. Olwen explains that her father will never consent to her marriage since her wedding presages Ysbaddaden's death. Nevertheless Culhwch approaches him and is given a series of 'impossible' tasks – reminiscent of the Labours of Hercules – which he must accomplish to win Olwen.

The most insuperable task forms the central core of the whole myth. This is the retrieval of the scissors, razor and comb from between the ears of one Twrch Trwyth, a huge, destructive boar who was once a king and who, to-gether with his followers, has been transformed by God as a punishment for his evil ways. Thus we meet the concept of transmogrification being imposed upon wrong-doers, just as occurs in 'Math'. In order to track down the great boar, Culhwch and Arthur have first to enlist the help of Mabon the Hunter, who is incarcerated in Gloucester Castle and of whom there has been no trace since he was stolen from his mother Modron as an infant. By the time Mabon is released from what must be an enchanted imprisonment, he is the oldest of all living creatures, a paradox for one named 'the Youth'. In this quest-within-a-quest for Mabon, Culhwch and Arthur are aided by magical animals: the Blackbird of Kilgowry; the Eagle of Gwernabwy; the Stag of Rhedenure; the Salmon of Llyn Llaw and other enchanted beasts, the most ancient animals on earth. One of Arthur's men, Gwrhyr, is able to communicate with these creatures in their own speech. With Mabon's help, Twrch Trwyth is finally overcome, after a chase which spans south Wales, Cornwall and Ireland. The razor, scissors and comb are delivered; Culhwch and Olwen finally marry.

Elements of the supernatural manifest themselves very clearly in *Culhwch and Olwen*. Culhwch's birth-link with pigs is developed in his final struggle against the great boar. The animal-theme is strong: enchanted and metamor-phosed beasts are prominent and contribute considerably to the outcome of the quest. Mabon the Hunter and Modron are overtly divine; the supernatural status of Culhwch himself is implied above all by his ability to threaten the future of Arthur's domain by imposing the curse of infertility on his people.

# The divine lovers

M any Celtic myths have as their central theme the love between two supernatural beings or between god and mortal, often with destructive results. A common pattern is the triangle of young lover, girl and unsuccessful (frequently elderly) suitor, and the jealousy which thus arises has damaging effects upon the land and its community. Irish myth also contains the theme of sacral kingship, whereby the union of king and goddess promotes the prosperity of the land. Interestingly the concept of divine love and marriage has a counterpart in the archaeological evidence for pagan Celtic religion: divine couples, represented both epigraphically and in the iconography, were venerated. In these cults the partnership itself seems to be symbolically significant and to produce harmony and prosperity.

## Love and jealousy in Irish myth

### Midhir and Étain

The *Book of Invasions* describes Midhir as lord of the *sīdh* (Otherworld mound) of Bri Léith, one of the Tuatha Dé Danann. One story of Midhir revolves around his love for a mortal girl, Étain. This excites the jealousy of Midhir's wife Fuamnach, who casts a spell on the girl, turning her first into a pool of water and then into a purple fly. Although Étain is mortal, she has certain supernatural powers, even in her transformed state. She can hum Midhir to sleep and warn him of an enemy's approach. Fuamnach conjures a magical wind which blows Étain away, but she is rescued and harboured by Oenghus, god of love, in his palace on the River Boyne. Oenghus' power is such that he can partially cancel the curse and Étain is restored to human form from dusk to dawn. But the hapless girl is then blown away once more and this phase of her life ends when she falls into a cup of wine belonging to the wife of the Ulster hero Edar. The wine is drunk and Étain is reborn as a new child, 1000 years on.

Midhir has maintained his quest for Étain over the 1000-year period. When he eventually discovers her, she is a grown woman, married to the king of Ireland. The god wins her back to him by means of trickery, managing to contrive a kiss, which causes Étain to remember him and love him once more. Midhir escapes with his love, having first transformed both of them into swans.

The character of Étain is interesting and betrays her superhuman status. She is reborn but retains her old identity 1000 years later; she is intimately linked

*Stone relief showing a genius cucullatus with an egg and a mother-goddess with fruit or bread, from Cirencester, Gloucestershire. The two deities are often associated in the Cotswold region. The egg is a powerful symbol of new life.*

with two deities, Oenghus and Midhir; and, most importantly, by her marriage to the Irish king, she fulfils the function of the goddess of sovereignty, validating his rule by their union. Midhir himself is a complex god, a lord of the Otherworld and a shape-shifter, but who requires a human mate whom he can endow with a status as elevated as his own.

## Oenghus and Caer

Oenghus of the Birds was an Irish god of love, one of the Tuatha Dé Danann. He is known as 'mac Oc' (the 'Young Son') because of the circumstances surrounding his birth to the Daghda and Boann. The divine pair concealed their illicit union and Boann's pregnancy by causing the sun to stand still in the heavens for nine months: so Oenghus was both conceived and born on the same day.

Oenghus' main role is as an aid to lovers in peril. Thus he intervenes in the plight of such couples as Midhir and Étain. But in 'The Dream of Oenghus' the god himself is smitten with an 'impossible' love. He dreams of a young girl whom he does not know. On waking he finds he is in love with her, and discovers her name to be Caer Ibormeith (Caer 'Yew-berry'). His search for her leads him to a lake where he finds Caer with her girl-companions. Caer is a shape-shifter: every other year, at the festival of Samhain (see page 55), she is transformed into a swan, together with her women. Oenghus observes that each pair of girls is joined by a silver chain, but Caer has a chain of gold. Caer's father refuses Oenghus' attentions to his daughter. The only way the two can marry is for Oenghus to take Caer when she changes to swan-shape. So, at Samhain, Oenghus approaches Caer's lake and flies off with her, having changed himself also to bird-form. The pair fly three times round the lake, their magical song sending everyone to sleep for three days and nights. The couple then fly to Oenghus' palace at Brugh na Bóinne.

Like the Welsh Mabon, Oenghus is the archetypal 'Young Man' or 'Divine Youth'. Caer is also of supernatural status: her father has his own *sídh* or Otherworld dwelling-place, and she has shape-changing powers. The image of enchanted swans, linked by chains of precious metal, is not confined to this myth but recurs, for instance, in tales associated with Cú Chulainn.

## Diarmaid and Gráinne

The story of Diarmaid ua Duibhne is chronicled in the Fionn Cycle. The elopement tale is first mentioned in the tenth-century *Book of Leinster*, and was incorporated into the Fionn Cycle at a later date. The tradition of Diarmaid's death occurs in compilations of the twelfth–fifteenth century. The tale of Diarmaid and Gráinne illustrates the recurrent theme of the mythic triangle: young girl, youth and jilted elderly suitor. Diarmaid is a lieutenant of Finn, ageing leader of the Fianna. Gráinne is betrothed to Finn but, at the pre-wedding feast, she sees Diarmaid and falls in love with him. Diarmaid is under a bond of loyalty to Finn and refuses Gráinne's advances, but she shames him by calling his honour as a man into question. The two flee from the royal court of Tara, and are pursued for many years by Finn. After seven years the old war-leader is apparently reconciled to the couple's union but the destructive result of the triangle is demonstrated by Finn's treachery towards Diarmaid. He invites his rival to take part in a boar-hunt, but he is aware of a prophecy that Diarmaid will meet his death in confrontation with this creature, the Boar of Boann Ghulban, who is in fact Diarmaid's enchanted foster-brother. There are two versions of the hero's death: in the first he is killed by the boar; in the second he overcomes the beast but dies when pierced by one of its poisonous bristles. Finn himself has the power to save Diarmaid by bringing him water cupped in his hands, but he hesitates and Diarmaid dies.

The fate of the couple is strongly bound up with the supernatural: the pair are aided in their trouble by Oenghus, who is Diarmaid's foster-father. He gives them advice in their wanderings, such as never to sleep two nights in one place. On their travels the couple enter the Forest of Duvnos, wherein is a Tree of Immortality, guarded by the Giant Sharvan. Though the monster is virtually immortal, Diarmaid slays him and both he and Gráinne eat the berries of the tree, thereby gaining near-immortality themselves. Diarmaid's death is only brought about by means of enchantment.

## Deirdre and Naoise

The ninth-century text which chronicles the ill-fated elopement of Deirdre and Naoise was later incorporated into the Ulster Cycle as a foretale of the *Táin*. King Conchobar of Ulster has a chief storyteller, Fedlimid, the father of

*Stone carving of a divine couple from Pagny-la-Ville, France. She has a patera (offering-plate) and he has a hammer and pot.*

Deirdre. Before her birth the court druid, Cathbadh, prophesies that the child will grow up to be beautiful but will bring ruin to the men of Ulster. Conchobar's warriors clamour for her death, but the king decides to rear her in secret and then marry her when she comes of age. When Deirdre is a young girl, still kept cloistered away from men, she observes Conchobar skinning a calf in the snow and a raven drinking the blood. She proclaims that the man she chooses will have the same three colours: black hair, white skin and red cheeks. Deirdre's companion Leabharcham comments that there is such a man, Naoise, son of Uisnech. The girl contrives to meet him but he is mindful of the prophecy and rejects her advances. Deirdre then challenges his honour (like Gráinne) and the pair elope, in the company of Naoise's two brothers, Ainle and Ardan.

The fugitives flee to Scotland, but are recalled to Emhain Macha with a false pardon sent by Conchobar. Only Deirdre suspects treachery. They return, and the three brothers are slain by one Eoghan. After keeping her captive for a year Conchobar plans to give Deirdre to Eoghan, but she kills herself rather than marry her lover's destroyer.

There are several points of mythological interest in this story. The doom-laden love-triangle of girl, youth and spurned suitor recurs. Deirdre herself is surrounded with mystery: the pre-birth prophecy about her effect upon Ulster, and the fact that it is because of her that three great heroes desert Conchobar's court (see pages 23–26); her own prophetic gift; her personality, which is stronger than that of Naoise, all raise Deirdre above normal human status. Naoise and his brothers are interesting: of the three only Naoise has any genuine identity. The brothers are mentioned perhaps to endow the story with triadic symbolism. Many of the Welsh and Irish myths contain references to 'three' as a magical or sacred number.

## The Welsh lovers

The Welsh lovers need be discussed only briefly here, since the relevant myths have been examined on pages 30–36. In the Welsh tradition two sets of lovers stand out as being of particular importance: Pwyll and Rhiannon in the First Branch of the *Mabinogi*, and Culhwch and Olwen, in the tale of that name. The story of Pwyll's wooing of Rhiannon contains elements which are comparable with those of the Irish tradition: it is Pwyll's trickery against Rhiannon's suitor Gwawl which causes the enchantment of Dyfed, chronicled in the Third Branch. The *Tale of Culhwch and Olwen* is somewhat different, but Culhwch's love causes momentous happenings and gives rise to the whole supernatural panoply of beings who appear in the myth. This love is not a herald of disaster, but it is strong enough to mobilise Arthur, Mabon and other larger-than-life individuals; and each task imposed upon Culhwch by Ysbaddaden can be accomplished only with divine help.

## Divine couples in pagan Celtic religion

The pairing of male and female deities was a prominent feature of the Celtic pantheon, as expressed in the iconography and epigraphy of Romano-Celtic Europe. A certain patterning can be discerned, in that when introduced to the Celtic world, gods of Graeco-Roman origin often acquired female consorts or partners who were indigenous to the conquered territory. So inscriptions frequently allude to a god with a Classical name linked to a Celtic-named goddess, an important example of this tradition being Mercury and Rosmerta. The male deity might have a Roman name but a Celtic epithet: such is the case with Apollo Grannus and Sirona. Alternatively both deities might be called by native names: Sucellus and Nantosuelta are good examples. Some divine couples were venerated over a wide area: Mercury and Rosmerta were worshipped in Britain, Gaul and the Rhineland. Others, like Ucuetis and Bergusia at Alesia, seem to have been invoked in only one place.

The symbolism associated with all the divine pairs worshipped in pagan Celtic Europe appears to show that the couples were invoked as promoters of health, wealth or abundance. Thus Sucellus (the 'Good Striker') and his consort Nantosuelta ('Winding Brook'), named on a stone at Sarrebourg in eastern Gaul, were particularly linked with the wine-harvest, especially in Burgundy. Sucellus' hammer struck the earth to fertilise it, and the domestic aspect to their cult is displayed by Nantosuelta's emblem of a house on a pole. Rosmerta's name means 'Great Provider', and the Celtic Mercury was invoked particularly as a bringer of commercial success, symbolised by his purse (a symbol that is Classical in origin) or money-chest. In Britain, Rosmerta has a vat or bucket whose symbolism may be regenerative like that of the cauldron of renewal so prominent in Irish and Welsh myth.

A number of the divine couples represented in Celtic imagery are associated with healing and protection. Thus the 'Celtic Apollo' and his various partners are strongly linked with cults of healing springs. Apollo and Sirona were worshipped at Hochscheid in Germany and elsewhere. Apollo Moritasgus and Damona were invoked at the springs of Alesia. Interestingly there was a close affinity between healing and fertility. Sirona and Damona, consorts of Apollo, are both symbolised with ears of corn and with serpents, which combine rebirth-imagery (because of the sloughing of their skins) with that of fecundity. At Hochscheid, Sirona carries eggs, powerful emblems of both fertility and regeneration. The goddesses sometimes reveal their 'polyandrous' nature: Damona, for instance, is coupled with Apollo at Alesia, with another healing god, Borvo, at Bourbonne-les-Bains, and with a local deity Abilus at Arnay-le-Duc, all in Gaul. Ancamna was the consort of the great healer Lenus Mars at Trier, but additionally of Mars Smertrius at Möhn, also in Treveran territory. The link between the Celtic Mars and healing seems to have derived from the idea of the god as a fighter/guardian against disease, barrenness and death.

Some divine couples were strictly territorial, personifications of the land or settlement where they were invoked. Such were Luxovius and Bricta at Luxeuil-les-Bains and Bormanus and Bormana at Die in France and Veraudinus and Inciona at Widdenburg in Luxembourg. This close tie with the land has a particular interest in connection with Insular mythical traditions of sacral kingship (see pages 18–20).

Whether or not it is sensible to attempt a link between the archaeological and vernacular evidence, what is clear from the iconography of divine couples is that the success of their cults lay, at least partly, in the marriage itself, and this may account for the popularity of divine couples throughout the Celtic world.

# The sky and sun myths

For many aspects of Celtic religion and myth, the literary sources are virtually silent, and it is necessary to turn to archaeology to fill in some of the gaps. The pagan Celts perceived numinosity (the presence of spirits) in all aspects of the natural world. Archaeological evidence suggests that, of all natural phenomena, the sun was especially invoked as a life-force, as a promoter of fertility and healing and as a comfort to the dead. It is difficult to construct a mythology or theology for the sun-cult by means of archaeological data alone, but some of the iconography which expresses solar invocation is sufficiently complex to allow some insight into the belief-systems which it represents.

## The vernacular tradition

In contrast with the material culture of pagan Celtic Europe, the evidence for a solar religion is sparse indeed when we turn to the Irish and Welsh vernacular myths. There are hints at a sun-cult, but they are indirect and indistinct. In Ireland the eponymous goddess Ériu possibly possessed a solar function, in her role as goddess of sovereignty, part of the ritual associated with sacral kingship. In a myth which grew up around the enactment of inaugural ritual, the sun is perceived as a golden cup full of red liquor (perhaps wine) borne by Ériu and handed to successive mortal kings of Ireland to legitimise or ratify their election and at the same time to promote the prosperity and fertility of the land. This myth is interesting for two reasons: first because the sun is associated with a goddess, in contrast to most sun-cults which are represented almost exclusively by male deities. In the pagan Celtic tradition as expressed by iconography, there is a solar goddess, represented by clay figurines, whose body is marked with sun-symbols. So there is a suggested link between the evidence of myth and of imagery. The second significant point concerns the Insular association between the sun and fecundity. This again is something which may be traced in the archaeological evidence for solar cults.

The veneration of the sun may be concerned with heat, light or both. If the light-element is emphasised, it may be difficult to distinguish between the sun and the sky as a source of cult. The Irish god Lugh ('Shining One') is clearly associated with brilliant light; he may or may not have been a sun-god, but his role as a divine young warrior, conqueror of evil, has its parallel in some of the pagan iconography considered below.

*Bronze figurine of the Celtic sky-god with his solar wheel, dedicated to Jupiter and the 'numen' of the Emperor, from Landouzy, France.*

The Welsh mythological tradition contains no overt evidence for a solar cult. However, there is one myth in which allusion to a god of light may be inferred. This is in 'Math', the Fourth Branch of the *Mabinogi*, which tells the story of the supernatural Lleu Llaw Gyffes (page 33). His name means 'Bright One of the Skilful Hand', and may be cognate with Lugh. Apart from his name, details of Lleu's behaviour also imply an association with celestial imagery. When struck by the spear of his wife Blodeuwedd's lover, Lleu changes into an eagle and flies into an oak tree. In pagan Romano-Celtic symbolism both the eagle and the oak were closely linked with the cult of the sky-god, whose Roman name was Jupiter.

## Sun-cults in pagan Celtic Europe

From as early as the middle of the Bronze Age, prehistoric communities in much of Europe venerated the sun and made its image in the form of the spoked wheel. The wheel-symbol was apparently chosen because of its shape and because of the element of movement common to both wheel and sun. In the early Iron Age clues as to the nature of celestial and solar religion are necessarily indirect, but certain repetitive behaviour is indicative of attitudes to the sun's power, as perceived by devotees. Warriors wore solar amulets as protection against harm in battle; people were buried in tombs accompanied by miniature sun-symbols, as if to illuminate their dark journey to the Otherworld. Worshippers offered model wheels in such shrines as that at Alesia in Burgundy, and cast them into rivers, such as the Seine, Oise and Marne, as votive offerings.

## The solar wheel-god

The Romano-Celtic period in Britain and Europe saw a great burgeoning of the solar religion. The evidence is for a multi-faceted, complex cult, the powers of the sun being perceived as having many functions and concerns. In this period the image of a sun-god, associated with his wheel-emblem, displayed Celtic perceptions of a solar power in human form. This was perhaps anticipated by the late Iron Age depiction of a wheel-god on the Danish Gundestrup Cauldron, which dates to the second–first century BC. The most prominent Romano-Celtic iconography represents the solar wheel-god as conflated, to an extent, with the imagery of the Roman sky-god Jupiter. A statuette of a wheel-bearing god from Landouzy in France, dedicated to Jupiter, expresses this tradition.

Interestingly the association between the sun and war, noted in the Iron Age, continues in the Romano-Celtic phase, when a distinctive group of images displays the solar/sky-god in battle against the forces of darkness and evil. These sculptures crown tall, tree-like pillars, known as 'Jupiter-Giant columns' because of their dedication to the Roman sky-god. Although the iconography of the victor riding down the foe may have its origins in Roman art, the images on the summit of these columns nonetheless depict a Celtic religious tradition, where the god of light and life is mounted on horseback, brandishing his protective solar wheel like a shield and his thunderbolt as a weapon, riding down the chthonic forces personified as a snake-limbed giant. The link between sun and war is not confined to Jupiter-columns. The north British war-god Belatucadrus has a name meaning 'Fair Shining One'; the Gaulish Mars Loucetius, invoked with his consort Nemetona at Bath, also bears a surname evocative of light. The pottery appliqué figure of a warrior-god at Corbridge (Northumberland) is accompanied by a wheel.

## The solar horse

Horses were closely linked to the solar cult. They were envisaged as animals of sufficient speed and prestige to carry the sky-god into battle, but their association with the sun is much more wide-ranging. In many Indo-European sun-myths, the solar disc was perceived as being carried across the sky in a chariot pulled by a horse-team. The chariot of the Greek god Apollo was the prototype for the reverse of many Celtic coins: Celtic artistry frequently reduced the image to a single horse, a chariot-wheel and a great spoked solar disc in the sky.

## Healing and fertility

The solar properties of heat and light gave rise to cults associated with the curing of disease and the promotion of abundance. Miniature sun-wheels were cast into curative springs; the goddess who presided over the great healing sanctuary at Bath was Sulis, a solar name. The Celtic Apollo was a deity of light and healing who was equated with a number of local gods and presided over many therapeutic spring shrines. Thus Apollo Belenus ('Bright' or 'Brilliant One') was venerated at such curative shrines as Sainte Sabine in Burgundy but also far away in Noricum (Austria). The name Belenus may have philological links with Beltene, the great Insular 1 May festival at which bonfires were lit in celebration of summer and as a purification rite to protect livestock from disease. Apollo Vindonnus, worshipped at Essarois in Burgundy, had a Celtic surname indicative of pure, clear light. It is significant that his cult was especially concerned with the curing of eye-afflictions. On the pediment of his temple was an image of Vindonnus as a radiate sun-god.

Fertility was seen as an important function for the divine sun, whose heat and light were clearly perceived as life-forces. The Celtic mother-goddesses were sometimes associated with the solar cult. Little clay figurines of goddesses from central Gaul and Brittany were depicted with solar symbols on their bodies. At Netherby in Cumbria and Naix in northern Gaul a deity is represented with a solar wheel and a *cornucopiae* (horn of plenty), a potent symbol of abundance.

## Fire

The great fire festivals of Celtic Europe took place in acknowledgement of fire as the terrestrial counterpart of the sun in the sky. Like the sun, fire both gives and destroys life. Fire is a cleanser, a purifier, and from ashes springs new, fertile vegetation. The fire-ceremonies were a form of sympathetic magic, enacted to persuade the sun to return after its winter desertion. Beltene on 1 May, Lughnasad on 1 August and Samhain at the end of the Celtic year (1 November) all celebrated critical times in the annual solar cycle (see 'Fertility, land and water', page 50). The Christian midsummer festival which marked the birth of St John the Baptist derived directly from much earlier ceremonies. Both pagan and

*The Felmingham Hall (Norfolk) hoard of Romano-British bronzes, including a model wheel.*

Christian festivals involved rolling a flaming wooden wheel down a hillside to a river. The Christian Saint Vincent observed a ceremony in fourth-century Aquitaine where a wheel was set alight, rolled to a river and then reassembled in the temple of the sky-god. A Saint John's festival, noted as being celebrated as late as the nineteenth century, records the rolling of a great, flaming, straw-covered wheel down the Stromberg Mountain to the River Moselle. If it reached the water unimpeded and without being quenched, a good wine-harvest was predicted. Thus the pagan association with fertility and plenty has long been maintained in an ostensibly Christian ritual.

## The sun and death

The supernatural power of the sun was perceived to penetrate the dark, infernal regions. During the Iron Age and Roman periods Celtic communities in Europe sometimes buried their dead with solar amulets, to comfort them in their sojourn in the Underworld. At the Dürrnberg in Austria, a deformed young girl, eight or ten years old but very stunted, was interred with a miniature bronze wheel-symbol: her burial is just one of many examples of this chthonic solar ritual. An even clearer link between death and the sun is demonstrated by a tradition which occurred in Romano-Celtic Alsace. Here tombstones were carved with solar designs which symbolically illuminated the gloom of the grave. The association between sunlight and the tomb may reflect the hope of rebirth in a happy Otherworld.

## Mountain-god and thunderer

High places are appropriate foci for the veneration of sky-forces. Mountains, penetrating sacred space, raised devotees as close as possible to the sky-god's element. Local Celtic mountain deities were equated with the Roman Jupiter: Ladicus was worshipped on Mount Ladicus in Spain; Poeninus in the high

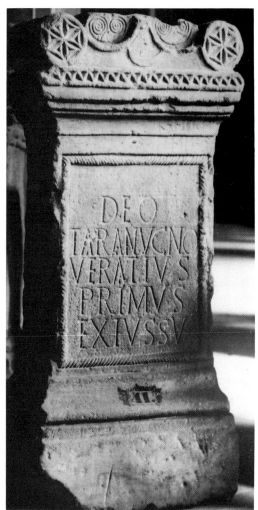

Romano-Celtic altar dedicated to Taranucnus, a derivative of Taranis the thunder god, from Böckingen, Germany.

Reconstructed Romano-Celtic Jupiter-Giant column, with horseman group at the summit, from Hausen-an-der-Zaber, Stuttgart, Germany.

Alpine passes of Gaul; Uxellinus in Austria. In the Pyrenees of south-west Gaul, a local version of Jupiter was venerated at such shrines as Le Mont Saçon and Valentine, and pilgrims dedicated small, roughly hewn altars, sometimes inscribed to Jupiter but decorated with wheels and swastikas. In this region the swastika was chosen as another sun-symbol, similar to the wheel but perhaps emphasising the concept of movement.

Mountain deities are frequently associated with weather and storms. The Syrian Jupiter Dolichenus is an example. The Celts had their own thunder-god Taranis, whose name derives from *taran*, a Celtic word for thunder. In the first century AD the Roman poet Lucan alludes in his *Pharsalia* to three terrifying Celtic gods, encountered by Caesar's army in Gaul:

> ... and those Gauls who propitiate with human sacrifices the merciless gods Teutates, Esus and Taranis – at whose altars the visitant shudders ....
> (trans. Robert Graves, Penguin, 1956)

A later glossator (commentator) on Lucan's poem links Taranis with the sacrifice of human beings in a gigantic flaming wicker man. Seven altars dedicated to this Celtic Thunderer are recorded in Romano-Celtic Europe: in Britain, at Chester; in Gaul; in the Rhineland and Dalmatia (the former Yugoslavia). On some of the dedications the god is called 'Jupiter Taranis'. Taranis is one element of celestial power, as the sun is another. But the solar wheel-god should not be perceived as the same entity as the Celtic Thunderer. Taranis represents the noisy, destructive, supernatural force of storms: his symbolism and identity are contained within the name itself.

## Cult and theology

That the cult of the Celtic sun/sky-gods may have had some kind of formalised ritual is implied by certain 'liturgical' finds. The temple at Wanborough in Surrey produced two chain headdresses surmounted by wheel-symbols, perhaps worn by priests of the sun-cult. The bronze mace from Willingham Fen (Cambridgeshire) with its depiction of the wheel-god also suggests ceremonial activity. Shrines, like that of Alesia in Burgundy, with its numerous model wheels, may have been consecrated to the sun-god.

Can we speak of a theology or mythology associated with the cults of sky and sun? Clearly, in the virtual absence of documentary detail, to speak of a celestial myth *sensu stricto* is incorrect. However, certain complex iconography demonstrates the one-time presence of a fundamental belief-system which must have been underpinned by myth. The sculptures of the Jupiter-columns hint at a dualistic, seasonal myth, where forces of day and night, light and darkness, life and death are balanced in an endless power struggle. The Willingham sceptre, with its figures of sun-god, three-horned bull, eagle, dolphin and infernal monster, exhibits a complexity which again argues for the presence of myth. Finally the whole range of material evidence shows the multiplicity of concerns of the celestial powers: life, healing, fertility and the mysteries of death and rebirth.

# Fertility, land and water

As is the case with many polytheistic systems, the Celtic gods were everywhere: each tree, lake, river, mountain and spring possessed a spirit. This concept of divinity in nature gave rise to many cults and myths associated with fertility. The most important of these were concerned with the mother-goddesses who presided over all aspects of plenty and prosperity, both in life and after death. In Irish mythology it was the union of the mortal king with the goddess of the land which promoted fertility in Ireland. The great Celtic festivals were all linked to the pastoral or agricultural year and the florescence of domestic animals and crops. Water was perceived as a life-force, and water-cults were a prominent feature of Celtic religion. Springs were the focus of curative cults based upon the healing and cleansing properties of pure water.

## Spirits in the landscape

The Celtic landscape was numinous (that is, possessed by spirits): the iconography and epigraphy of Romano-Celtic Europe attest to the sanctity of natural places, which were perceived to be under the protection of local divinities. A settlement and its god might even share the same name: thus, in southern Gaul, Glanis was the spirit of Glanum and Nemausus was the name both of Nîmes and of the god who presided over the sacred spring. Mountains were holy and their spirits venerated: Vosegus was the god of the Vosges in eastern Gaul; and Ladicus, the eponymous spirit of Mount Ladicus in north-west Spain, has been alluded to on page 47.

Trees, groves and forests were sacred. The symbolism of trees is complex: their roots and branches evoked an image of a link between sky and Underworld; their longevity represented continuity and wisdom; the seasonal behaviour of deciduous trees gave rise to a cyclical symbolism, an allegory of life, death and rebirth. Trees were associated with cults of fertility and nature, partly because of this regenerative imagery: the mother-goddesses are frequently associated with trees; Rhenish altars to the mother-goddesses from Bonn bear tree-symbols; the sanctuary of the mothers at Pesch (Germany) had a sacred tree as its cult-focus. Gaulish tribal names display tree-veneration: the Eburones were the 'Yew Tribe', the Lemovices the 'People of the Elm'. In Ireland a sacred tree was called a *bile*; the older the tree, the greater its sanctity. All trees in Irish myth were sacred but the oak, yew, ash and hazel were particularly

*Romano-Celtic stone mother-goddess figurine with a tree, corn (or palm) branch symbol and fruit, from Caerwent, South Wales.*

holy. In the *Dinnshenchas* allusion is made to trees as sources of sacred wisdom. Irish holy trees were associated with sacral kingship: the inauguration of a ruler always took place in the presence of a sacred tree, a symbol of sovereignty, tradition and wisdom. A group of trees (a grove) was equally sacred, called *fidnemed* in Ireland and *nemeton* by the Gauls and Britons.

## Cults of water and curative springs

Water was perceived as both a creator and destroyer of life. Thus water in all its aspects – particularly rivers, springs, wells, lakes and marshes – was the focus of countless myths and cults which manifest themselves both in archaeology and in the western literature. The sanctity and symbolism of water continued into the Christian tradition. Rivers were regarded as a numinous life-force: from as early as the Bronze Age, people cast precious objects into them as votive offerings. In the Celtic Iron Age, rivers such as the Thames and Witham received particularly martial items: weapons, armour and shields. Rivers at their sources and confluences were especially holy. Condatis ('Watersmeet') was venerated in the Tyne-Tees region of north Britain, and 'Condate' at Lyon was the sacred site at the confluence of the great Rhône and Saône rivers. There is evidence that the *personae* of many rivers were worshipped as named spirits: Sequana of the Seine; Souconna of the Saône; Verbeia of the Wharfe are just a few examples. The Insular *Dinnshenchas* relates the myth of the River Boyne, personified as the goddess Boann, who was turned into a river as a punishment by her husband Nechtan, himself a water-spirit, for daring to visit his forbidden well (Sídh Nechtan).

Lakes and marshes were equally numinous. The Classical writer Strabo testifies to the deposition of treasure in sacred lakes, and there is archaeological evidence for this practice. At the Swiss lake-site of La Tène, wooden platforms (some dated by dendrochronology to the second century BC) were specially built to facilitate the casting of precious objects into a small bay at the eastern end of Lake Neuchâtel. Offerings included hundreds of brooches, weapons and shields, chariots and animals, thrown in over a period which centred around 100 BC. In Wales the lake of Llyn Fawr in Mid Glamorgan was the centre of cult-activity in about 600 BC, when objects including antique cauldrons and exotic material of the style known as Hallstatt (from the type-site in Austria), were deposited. Llyn Cerrig Bach on Anglesey was a watery site into which had been cast many prestige objects, including chariots, weapons and cauldrons, over a period from the second century BC to the first century AD. It is possible that Llyn Cerrig was associated with the druids, described by the Roman writer Tacitus as having an important cult-centre on the Island of Mona.

The repeated deposition of cauldrons in water is interesting. These vessels were traditionally associated with feasting and plenty, in vernacular myth. The Irish god the Daghda possessed an enormous, ever-replenishing cauldron (pages 15–16); and the Welsh hero Brân (pages 31–2) gave a cauldron of rebirth to the Irish king Matholwch. Their function as containers for liquid may be the reason why they were so often deposited as sacred offerings in watery contexts. The great Danish Brå and Gundestrup Cauldrons were found in marshes; the Duchcov (Czechoslovakia) Cauldron came from a Celtic spring sanctuary and held more than 2000 items of bronze jewellery. Scottish lakes, such as Carlingwark Loch and Blackburn Mill, were the focus of ritual cauldron deposition in the very late Iron Age (early first century AD).

Bogs were the centre of important cult activity, not only because of their watery nature but also perhaps because of the element of danger and treachery

*Late Iron Age bronze cauldron found with a second vessel inverted over it, and deposited as a votive gift in a marsh at Blackburn Mill, Scotland.*

associated with them. In the Celtic Iron Age the marsh-spirits were propitiated with offerings ranging from weapons, cauldrons and wagons to human sacrifices. The Scottish Torrs Chamfrein, an elaborate item of horse-armour, came from a marsh, as did the Gundestrup Cauldron and two cult-wagons from Dejbjerg in Denmark. The most spectacular marsh-offering from Britain was found at Lindow Moss, the body of a young man who was garotted and cast naked into a marsh-pool some time during the Iron Age (see page 68).

Springs and wells were associated with divinities and especially with cults of healing. Wells, which penetrated deep below ground, were perceived as a link between the earth and the Underworld. The goddess Coventina presided over a sacred spring and well at the Roman fort of Carrawburgh on Hadrian's Wall. A Romano-British well at Goadby, Leicestershire, contained the bodies of two people, weighted down with stones, perhaps offerings to the infernal powers. A dry well dating to the Roman period at Jordan Hill, Dorset, contained very curious and deliberately structured deposits, including stone cists filled with ironwork and sixteen pairs of tiles between each of which were the body of a crow and a coin. Sacred wells feature in Insular myths: the Fionn Cycle describes the Salmon of Knowledge which lived at the bottom of a well. The cult of the Irish goddess Brigit, who became a Christian saint, was closely associated with sacred wells. Many saints presided over holy wells: St Melor of Cornwall is an example. Saint Winifride's Well at Holywell in Clwyd is one of many in Wales. As is the case with the legend of the Welsh Saint Winifride, the severed heads of Breton saints endowed particular wells with sanctity and power.

Springs were revered in acknowledgement of their medicinal and purifying properties. In Romano-Celtic times powerful cults associated with healing springs attracted pilgrims from all over Celtic Europe. The two natural springs at Chamalières near Clermont-Ferrand possess minerals with genuine curative properties: in the first century BC and first century AD the sacred pool was visited by sick devotees who offered to the presiding spirit wooden images of themselves, displaying particularly eye-afflictions. In the same period a shrine at *Fontes Sequanae* (the Springs of Sequana) was established near Dijon, in veneration of the healing goddess of the Seine at its spring-source. More than 200 wooden models of pilgrims, or the parts of their bodies which required a cure, were dedicated to the goddess. Healing cults like this were based upon the principle of reciprocity: after bathing in the pure, sacred water of the spring, the devotee offered a model of a diseased limb or organ, in the hope that the deity would give back one that was whole and healthy.

Many other curative spring deities were worshipped in Gaul and Britain: the Celtic Apollo presided over many of these sites, sometimes with a consort (see pages 41–2). As Apollo Belenus he was venerated at Sainte Sabine in Burgundy and elsewhere; Apollo Grannus, with his consort Sirona, was invoked at Grand (Vosges), but his shrines existed as far apart as Brittany and Hungary. Here, as in other shrines, sick suppliants bathed, offered their gifts and then slept in a special dormitory, where they hoped for a vision of the healing god. Other powerful healers included Lenus Mars, a Treveran god whose main cult-centre was associated with a stream and spring near the Moselle at Trier. The greatest British curative deity was Sulis, whose sanctuary was at Aquae Sulis, the great temple at Bath, established on a site where hot springs gush from the ground at the rate of a quarter million gallons (1,136,500 litres) a day.

## Myths and cults of fertility

The Celts were an essentially rural people and, as such, were preoccupied with the seasons and with the fertility and well-being of their crops and livestock. Most of the divinities of Celtic Europe, who were associated with the natural world, had a function as providers of fertility: Cernunnos, Epona, the hunter-gods and the healers are just a few examples. Cloaked and hooded spirits, known as *Genii Cucullati*, are represented in iconography carrying such evocative symbols as eggs. Continental examples may display overt sexual symbolism: on some images the hood can be removed to expose an erect phallus. The British *Cucullati* are distinctive in their triple form and in their repeated association with depictions of the mother-goddesses.

It is the Mothers who most clearly display the concept of the personification of fertility. The earth-mother, provider of abundance, was a fundamental aspect of divinity for the European Celts (as, indeed, was the case in Classical lands and elsewhere in the ancient world). This concept bears close resemblance to that expressed in the Irish and Welsh image of goddesses such as Macha, Medb and Modron. The cult of the divine mother was popular all over Romano-Celtic Europe: she was depicted most frequently as a triad, and epigraphy too expresses this plurality, referring to the goddesses as the *Deae Matres* or *Deae Matronae*. This triplism seems to occur most frequently in the imagery of divine beings associated with prosperity and well-being. The Mothers most often appear seated in a row, with such symbols of fertility as babies, fruit or bread. A typical Burgundian image, exemplified by a relief at Vertault, shows the goddesses with a baby, a napkin or towel and a sponge and basin. The Germanic *Matronae* were topographical goddesses, with local surnames such as the *Aufaniae*. They carry fruit rather than emblems of human fertility, but are distinctive in that their images always depict two older goddesses flanking a young girl, as if the different ages of womanhood are expressed. The British mother-goddesses are depicted both with children and fruit or bread; they cluster in two geographical groups, that of the West Country and that of Hadrian's Wall.

## The Celtic festivals

Four great seasonal religious festivals are recorded in Insular mythic tradition, all associated with the farming year. Imbolc, celebrated on 1–2 February, was related to the lactation of ewes. This festival was linked with the cult of Brigit, a multi-functional goddess who protected women in childbirth, presided over the

*Romano-Celtic pipe-clay group of the three mother-goddesses, from Bonn, Germany. The Rhenish mothers almost invariably follow this iconographic pattern, with a young girl flanked by two older women with distinctive headdresses.*

ale-harvest and was also associated with poetry and prophecy. Interestingly Brigit retained many of her pagan roles even when she had been adopted as a saint by the early Celtic Church in Ireland.

The feast of Beltene ('Bright- or Goodly-Fire') took place on 1 May; it was related to the beginning of open pasturing, and was celebrated to welcome summer and the heat of the sun which would ripen the crops. Bonfires were kindled in sympathetic magic to encourage the sun's warmth on earth. The ninth century AD glossator Cormac describes a Beltene ritual in which two fires were ignited by the druids and livestock driven between them in a magical ritual of fertility and purification.

Lughnasad was linked with the harvest. Its central date of celebration was 1 August, but the festivities lasted a month. According to Irish tradition, the fair of Lughnasad was introduced by Lugh to Ireland, either in memory of his foster-mother Tailtu or to celebrate his marriage. The festival was held at various locations, including the royal strongholds of Tara and Emhain Macha.

Samhain (31 October/1 November) is the festival about which most is known. It marked the beginning of winter and the Celtic new year. Samhain heralded the time in the pastoral year when animals were brought in from the fields, some slaughtered and others kept for breeding. Samhain is recorded on the first century BC Gaulish Coligny Calendar (see page 64) as 'Samonios'. In Ireland during the later first millennium AD great assemblies of the five provinces took place at Samhain, occasions for pastoral rites and political debate: the festival was celebrated with markets, fairs and horse-races. Samhain was a time of ritual mourning for the death of summer and a period of great danger, a boundary between two periods, when time and space were temporarily frozen and normal laws suspended. The barriers were broken: Otherworld spirits could walk on earth and humans could visit the Underworld. The tradition of Samhain has survived into modern times as Hallow'een and All Souls' Day.

# Animals in cult and myth

Animals were revered by the Celts, as by many non-Christian cultures, for their specific qualities: speed, ferocity, fecundity, valour or beauty. The behaviour of certain beasts gave rise to religious symbolism: the earthbound nature of snakes led to perceptions of links between these creatures and the Underworld; the ability of birds to fly was seen in terms of an allegory of the human spirit freed at death. An important element in sacred myth was the absence of rigid boundaries between animal and human form. This meant that, in iconography, deities could be envisaged as semi-zoomorphic. The myths of the vernacular literature abound in enchanted animals which had once been human, and divinities in human form who could shape-change to the form of an animal at will. Apart from the evidence of images and myths, the importance of animals in Celtic ritual is clearly demonstrated by the complexity and diversity of animal sacrifice.

## Wild beasts and the hunt

Although wild animals were not a major food-source, hunting was a common sporting and prestige activity. The divine hunt forms an important part of vernacular myth, and the iconography of the pagan Celtic world displays a multiplicity of cults associated with hunted animals.

There existed a special and complicated relationship between the Celts and the creatures they hunted, a relationship that involved reverence and an acknowledgement of theft from the natural world, which required appropriate propitiatory ritual. The gods of the hunt protected the denizens of the wild as well as promoting the hunt itself. Sometimes this ambivalence is displayed in Celtic imagery, where the god shows tenderness toward his prey: the sculpture of the hunter-god with his stag from Le Donon (Vosges) is a good example. Many divine hunters are accompanied by dogs, just as would have been the case in real life.

The concept of the divine hunt possesses important regenerative symbolism. The spilling of the blood of the hunted means food and life for the hunters. In the Welsh and Irish mythological tradition the hunt may be the means by which contact is made between earthly life and the Otherworld. In Irish myth beings from the supernatural world lured human hunters, such as Finn, to their realm by means of enchanted animals. In the *Mabinogi*, it is a stag-hunt which brings together Pwyll and the Otherworld king, Arawn.

*Stone statuette of a god wearing a torc, from Euffigneix, France. He has an eye-symbol on his side, perhaps to indicate the all-seeing power of the god, and a boar striding along his torso, dorsal bristles erect. The boar image suggests hunting or war symbolism.*

Certain deities were associated with particular hunted animals. Bears were protected by Artio, a goddess worshipped near Bern in Switzerland, where a bronze statuette depicts her and her beast. Arduinna, a divine huntress of the Ardennes Forest, is portrayed on a bronze figurine astride a galloping boar, a hunting-knife in her hand. A pre-Roman carving from Euffigneix in eastern Gaul shows a god with the image of an aggressively bristled boar striding along his torso. The bellicosity suggested by the raised dorsal crest is emphasised on figurines of boars, such as that from Neuvy-en-Sullias (Loiret). Celtic helmets and shields carried boar-emblems as war-symbols, and the *carnyx* (war-trumpet) was fashioned with a snarling boar's head as its mouthpiece. The focus of the Welsh tale of *Culhwch and Olwen* is Twrch Trwyth, a huge, destructive boar (see page 35), and similar beasts are common in Irish myth: Orc Triath is the equivalent of Twrch Trwyth.

Stags were important cult-animals, probably because of their speed, their virility and their spreading antlers, which evoked their image as lords of the forest. The Iron Age rock-art of Camonica Valley in north Italy features sacred stags which are often depicted as the focus of hunting-ritual. The imagery on a seventh-century-BC model bronze cult-wagon at Strettweg in Austria is of a divine stag-hunt presided over by a goddess. In later Celtic iconography the deer is the companion not only of hunter-gods but also of the god Cernunnos, who was himself antlered (see below). Supernatural stags are significant in vernacular myth. In the Fionn Cycle, Finn himself is closely associated with deer-imagery: his wife, Sava, is a metamorphosed doe and the name of their son, Oisin, means 'Little Deer'. Finn is one of the hunters enticed to the Otherworld by means of enchanted stags.

## Snakes and birds

The complex symbolism of the snake arises from its physical characteristics: its habit of sloughing its skin has caused it to be perceived as a symbol of rebirth, hence its association with healer-deities such as Sirona. In Classical religion, serpents were symbols of beneficence and also of death. Snakes were linked with fertility-imagery, perhaps because of their phallic shape, the double penis of the male and the multiple young produced at one birth. The snake's earthbound nature, its carnivorous feeding-habits and its ability to kill gave it powerful chthonic symbolism. This is displayed most clearly in the iconography of the Jupiter-columns (see page 45), where the monster of darkness is represented by a Giant with serpents replacing his legs. One distinctive form of snake-iconography consists of the ram-headed serpents: these occur particularly in Romano-Celtic Gaul. The symbolism is generally interpreted as representative of the combined imagery of fertility (the ram was symbolic of fecundity in the Classical world) and regeneration. These hybrid creatures often accompany beneficent deities of abundance or healing: Cernunnos and the Celtic equivalent of Mercury or Mars in his Gaulish role as guardian against misfortune are examples.

Snakes feature in a number of Irish myths. This itself is interesting because, since there are no snakes in Ireland, the implication must be that these snake-myths are of great antiquity. The war-fury, the Morrigán, has a son, Meiche, who is slain by Dian Cécht, the divine physician, because he has three snakes in his heart. There was a prophecy that, if the serpents were allowed to mature, they would destroy all the animals in Ireland. The Ulster champion Conall Cernach has an encounter with a great treasure-guarding snake. The Welsh cleric Giraldus Cambrensis wrote an account of a gold torc guarded by a snake in a Pembrokeshire well. The theme of a treasure-guarding serpent is widespread in European legend: it has its equivalent, for instance, in Fafnir of Norse myth.

Apart from their general symbolism associated with flight, birds possessed other, more specific, symbolism. Their distinctive 'voices' may have led to the oracular associations of ravens and doves. Water-birds may have been seen as a symbolic link between sky and water. The alert and protective character of geese led to their symbolic connection with war. In both Irish and Welsh tradition, magical birds, usually in threes, were associated with healing and rebirth in the Otherworld. The bright-plumaged birds of the Irish goddess Clíodna and the birds of the Welsh Rhiannon could lull the sick to sleep with their sweet song.

Cranes were important in Irish myth: those belonging to Midhir were birds of ill omen, whose presence robbed warriors of their courage. Ill-natured or jealous women were punished by being changed into cranes: this idea may have come about because the crane's raucous shriek was likened to the screech of a scold. The Irish sea-god Manannán possessed a bag made from the skin of a crane which had once been a jealous woman. That cranes or egrets were significant also in Gaulish religion is demonstrated by the curious iconography of Tarvostrigaranus, the 'Bull with Three Cranes', depicted on stones at Paris and Trier dating from the first century AD.

As eaters of carrion and with their black plumage, crows and ravens were particularly associated with death. Irish war-goddesses such as the Morrigán and Badbh could assume crow-form and appear on the battlefield as harbingers of disaster. In Insular myth the prophetic associations of ravens were usually related to the foretelling of evil. Ravens and crows were important symbols in pagan European iconography, but here they seem to have been linked to beneficent deities, like Nantosuelta, Epona and the healers, perhaps as prophets of good fortune. Ritual involving ravens occurred in the British Iron Age: at Danebury and Winklebury in Hampshire, bodies of ravens were deliberately buried in pits, perhaps as sacrifices to the infernal powers.

Other birds which were important in myth included eagles and swans. In iconography the eagle was associated above all with sky-symbolism. In Welsh myth the eagle is linked with Lleu Llaw Gyffes, perhaps a god of light (see page 35). Irish myth abounds in stories of enchanted swans, which spend some time as birds and some as girls: stories about Midhir and Étain, Oenghus and Caer (see 'The divine lovers', page 37) and Cú Chulainn all carry descriptions of magical swans wearing gold or silver chains, apparently a mark of their supernatural status. In one myth the children of Lir (a sea-god) are cursed with swan-shape for 900 years because of the jealousy of their stepmother. The particular association of swans with lovers may derive from the observation that swans mate for life.

## Epona and horses

Horses were prestige animals, used for riding from at least the eighth century BC in 'barbarian' Europe. They had long been used to pull wagons, but the Celts had two-horse teams to draw light, fast chariots in battle. The horse was revered in the Celtic world for its beauty, speed, bravery and sexual vigour, and this animal became a symbol of the aristocratic warrior-élite of Celtic society, the knights. Many cults were associated with horses: warrior-gods, such as Mars Corotiacus at Martlesham in Suffolk, were depicted in iconography on

*Small bronze group of Epona (above left) and two ponies, from Wiltshire. The goddess has a yoke and a dish of corn from which the animals feed. Romano-Celtic.*

*Large stone monument of Nehalennia (above right), shown with dog and fruit-baskets, from Colijnsplaat, Netherlands.*

horseback; and there is evidence, too, that the horse was perceived as a solar animal (page 46). Horse sacrifice was rare, but significant in its reflection of a very real loss to its owner and the community. The quartered bodies of two horses were found in a ritual deposit of the sixth century BC in the cave of Býčiskála in Czechoslovakia; and the later Iron Age chariot-burial of the King's Barrow in East Yorkshire contained the horse-team as well as the chariot and its owner.

Greatest of all the Celtic horse-deities was Epona, her very name philologically linked with *epos*, a Celtic word for horse. She was sufficiently important to have an official Roman festival, on 18 December. Epona's worshippers were drawn from all sections of society: in military areas of the Rhine and Danube she was venerated by cavalry officers of the Roman army, as a protectress of both horseman and animal. Elsewhere, especially in Burgundy, Epona was worshipped as a domestic deity, goddess of the craft of horse-breeding and, more generally, of abundance and prosperity. Her imagery is distinctive: she is always depicted in company with horses, either riding side-saddle on a mare or between two or more horses or ponies. The female sex of her mount may be important in terms of her role as promoter of fertility: Burgundian images frequently portray a sleeping or suckling foal beneath Epona's mare. The horse-goddess was essentially a Gaulish divinity, although dedications occur as far away as Plovdiv in Bulgaria. There is little evidence for Epona's cult in Britain, but a bronze statuette from Wiltshire shows the goddess with two ponies, a male and a female, whom she feeds with corn.

Irish and Welsh mythology contains a great deal of horse-symbolism: Macha, an Irish horse-goddess, outran the Ulster king's team in a race; and the Welsh Rhiannon had a close affinity with horses, and may herself have been a horse-goddess.

## The symbolism of dogs

In both Classical and Celtic myth, dogs possessed the complex but symbiotic symbolism of healing, hunting and death, derived from observation of the self-healing power of a dog's lick, its scavenging habits and its role in hunting. Dogs played an important part in Welsh and Irish myth: Arawn, lord of Annwn (the Welsh Otherworld) possessed supernatural hounds, described in the *Mabinogi* as white with red ears. The 'Taliesin' poem *Cwn Annwn* (the *Hounds of Annwn*) refers to speckled, greyish-red dogs which are omens of death. The Ulster hero Cú Chulainn has a close link with dogs. Named the 'Hound of Culann', he takes the place of the smith's great hound, whom he has killed; he also has a *geis* or bond which forbids him to eat dog-flesh. Mac Da Thó, who presides over an Irish Otherworld feast, has an enormous and supernatural hound, whom he offers both to the men of Ulster and of Connacht, thus promoting their mutual hatred.

In pagan Celtic Gaul and Britain there is evidence of dog-ritual and sacrifice. At Danebury in Hampshire dogs (often in association with horses) were killed and interred in disused grain-storage pits during the Iron Age; at the pre-Roman shrine of Gournay (Oise), dogs were consumed in ritual meals. Many deities venerated in pagan Celtic Europe were associated with dogs. Hunter-gods are depicted accompanied by large hounds. Apollo Cunomaglus ('Hound Lord') was invoked at the sanctuary of Nettleton in Wiltshire. The great Romano-Celtic shrine at Lydney, Gloucestershire, was presided over by Nodens, a god who received offerings of dog-images. The marine goddess Nehalennia presided over two temples on the North Sea coast of the Nether-lands, at Colijnsplaat and Domburg, both now submerged beneath the sea. More than a hundred images of the goddess have survived, nearly all of which depict her accompanied by a large, watchful hound. Nehalennia was a divinity who protected travellers across the North Sea and promoted their success in business. The baskets of fruit which accompany her suggest that she was a goddess of plenty. The dog may be a symbol of protection and fidelity.

## Tarvostrigaranus and the bull myths

Bulls were venerated for their strength, their virility and roaring ferocity. Oxen were symbolic of the power of draught-animals in farming, and thus of agricul-tural wealth. Bull sacrifice was not uncommon: elderly oxen were ritually slaughtered at Gournay, and their bodies subjected to elaborate rites. In his

*Natural History*, the Roman writer Pliny refers to a druidical bull-sacrifice.

Sacred bulls are frequently represented in cult-art: figurines of the sixth century BC have been found at Hallstatt in Austria and Býčiskála. Celtic bull-images are often depicted triple-horned, thus enhancing the symbolism of the horn (which signified aggression and fertility) to the sacred power of three. Stone triple-horned bulls were dedicated at the Burgundian shrine of Beire-le-Châtel; and bronze examples occur in Gaul and in Britain. One figurine of the fourth century AD comes from a shrine at Maiden Castle, Dorset, and once was adorned with images of three women on its back. In Irish legend women were sometimes transformed into cranes, and the Maiden Castle figurine calls to mind some curious Continental iconography dating to the first century AD: one carving, from Paris, depicts a bull with three cranes perched on its back and head; the accompanying dedication reads 'Tarvostrigaranus' (the 'Bull with Three Cranes'). Almost identical imagery is present on a stone at Trier. Both stones depict the bull and birds associated with willow trees and a divine wood-cutter. The interpretation is obscure, but some scholars have advanced theories of seasonal symbolism, related to the Tree of Life, spring and fertility. This imagery may well represent a quite specific Celtic myth, the details of which have been lost.

Bull-myths are very prominent in early Irish literature. The *tarbhfhess* was a divinatory rite involving a bull sacrifice, presided over by druids (see 'Druids, sacrifice and ritual', page 62); the bull's flesh and broth were consumed by a man who then slept and dreamed of the rightful king-elect. The most important Irish bull-myth is the *Táin Bó Cuailnge* in the Ulster Cycle (page 21).

## Zoomorphism and shape-shifting

The close religious affinity between Celts and animals manifests itself most clearly in two ways: the first concerns the representation of gods in semi-zoomorphic form; the second is metamorphosis or shape-changing, which is such a common concept in the Welsh and Irish mythological tradition.

A carving of the first century AD from Paris (part of the same monument as the Tarvostrigaranus stone) depicts the bust of an elderly man with antlers, a torc hanging from each, and the ears of a stag. The inscription above identifies him as 'Cernunnos' ('Horned One'). Similar images occur in both pre-Roman and Romano-Celtic contexts. The earliest representation is on a fourth-century-BC rock-carving at Camonica Valley in north Italy. The antlered god appears on the Gundestrup Cauldron, seated cross-legged, again with two torcs, and with his stag beside him. Beneath the god is a ram-horned serpent. Most images of Cernunnos occur in north-east Gaul and date to the Roman period. He is often depicted as he is at Gundestrup, cross-legged, with torcs and a horned snake. At such sites as Sommerécourt and Étang-sur-Arroux in Gaul the snakes eat from bowls of mash on the god's lap. A rare British example, at Cirencester, portrays Cernunnos with two snakes which form his legs and rear up to eat corn or fruit by his head. Some Gaulish images have holes in the top of the head for detach-

*Bronze bull-head bucket-mount (above right) from Welshpool, Wales. Late Iron Age.*

*Bust of a god (above left) with antlers and torcs hanging from them; above is a dedication to Cernunnos. Early first century AD, from Nôtre Dame, Paris, France.*

able antlers, possibly evoking seasonal ritual. The general symbolism of Cernunnos is that of a wild god of nature, fertility and plenty. He is so close to the animal world that he actually takes on some characteristics of a beast, thus enhancing his potency as lord of Nature.

Essentially similar to Cernunnos are the horned gods, who adopt the features of bulls, rams or goats. These are especially popular among the Brigantes of north Britain, where they frequently appear as ithyphallic warrior-gods, thus linking sexual vigour with military aggression.

A strong and persistent thread running through the earliest written Celtic myths is the concept of enchanted, magical animals which may be of supernatural origin, perhaps metamorphosed gods or humans who have been changed into animals in revenge or as a punishment. This chapter has already touched upon such transmogrified beings as Twrch Trwyth, changed from a human king to a boar because of his wickedness; the various beings who change into swans; and the Irish raven-goddesses. In the *Mabinogi*, Gwydion and Gilfaethwy are transformed into a succession of animals by Math, lord of Gwynedd. Irish mythology is full of enchanted bulls, boars, stags and birds. A constant characteristic of all transmogrified creatures is that only their physical form is altered; they retain the ability to think as humans and they can often still speak. They are skin-changers, very similar to those of Norse myth.

In addition to gods or humans who can assume zoomorphic form, the western Celtic myths contain allusions to special animals with supernatural powers. Thus the Welsh Culhwch encounters magical creatures who help him in his quest. One of these is the Salmon of Llyn Llaw, a creature which bears a close resemblance to the Irish Salmon of Knowledge, chronicled in the Fionn Cycle, whose flesh imparts wisdom to the young Finn. This salmon gained its knowledge by eating the nuts of the nine hazel trees which grew beside a well at the bottom of the sea, in other words from the Otherworld.

# Druids, sacrifice and ritual

This book is about myth and its prime concern is to explore stories and beliefs about the supernatural world. Nevertheless it is important also to consider the 'mechanics' of Celtic religion which underpin the myths and belief-systems themselves. This chapter therefore examines aspects of ritual behaviour, the performance of people who wished to communicate with that separate world beyond the boundaries of human perception.

## Druids, seers, bards: an international Celtic priesthood?

The Druids are engaged in sacred matters, conduct the public and private sacrifices, and interpret all religious issues. To these a large number of the young men resort for the purpose of instruction, and the Druids are held in great honour among them.
(trans. Wiseman and Wiseman, *The Battle for Gaul*, Chatto and Windus, 1980)

A number of Classical writers mention the druids: Strabo, Tacitus, Lucan and Ausonius are but a few. The fullest information is given by Caesar, whose words are quoted above. He comments that the druids enjoyed high rank, being of nearly equal status with the knights. He speaks of the rigours of the druids' training, which could take twenty years and involved committing to memory oral traditions passed on through the generations. Every year, on a fixed date, the druids assembled in a sacred place in the land of the Carnutes, the official centre of Gaul. Caesar makes it clear that druidism originated in Britain whence it was disseminated to Gaul. Most Graeco-Roman sources agree that the main concern of the druids was the control of supernatural forces by means of divination. This apparently involved human sacrifice by stabbing, strangulation or other means, and the examination of the death struggles or the victim's innards in order to foretell the future.

Tacitus alludes to divinatory killing on the Island of Anglesey when it was threatened by invading Romans. This magical prediction made it possible to plan the most auspicious time for important events in the community: going to war, sowing or reaping, election of a new king and so forth. The first-century-BC Gaulish Coligny Calendar is one the earliest surviving pieces of evidence for a written (using Roman letters) Celtic language. It consists of a large bronze plate engraved with a calendar of lunar and intercalary months, each divided into lucky and unlucky halves, demarcated by the abbreviations MAT (good) and ANM (not good). It is possible that this was a calendar drawn up by the druids in order to calculate propitious times for important religious and secular

*Bronze priest's crown (above left) from the Romano-Celtic temple of Hockwold-cum-Wilton, Norfolk.*

*Lifesize Romano-Celtic pewter mask (above right), perhaps nailed onto the door of a shrine, found in the culvert of the sacred baths of Sulis at Bath.*

activities. Pliny chronicles a druidic sacrifice associated with the curing of barrenness: on the sixth day of the moon the druids climbed a sacred oak and cut off a mistletoe bough using a 'golden' (probably gilded-bronze) sickle, catching the branch in a white cloak. Two white bulls were then sacrificed. When mixed in a potion, mistletoe was believed to cure infertility.

Druids were probably very influential in religion and politics during the free Celtic period – perhaps all over the Celtic world, though we have evidence only for Gaul and Britain – but, as an active force, druidism would have gradually faded under Roman domination. Some early emperors tolerated the druids; others tried to eradicate them. The Bordeaux poet Ausonius alludes to the presence of druids in Gaul during the fourth century AD. But when the main fabric of Celtic heroic society broke down, so did most of the druids' influence. There is no archaeological evidence for druids *per se* but some liturgical regalia – headdresses and sceptres – does survive. The excavators of the Celtic sanctuary of Gournay in northern Gaul suggest the presence of a permanent staff of religious functionaries to maintain the ritual activity evidenced there. Whether these officials were druids is, of course, an open question.

Irish mythology abounds in references to druids, although they must have lost most of their power under Christianity. In the *Book of Invasions* one of the invading leaders, Partholón, arrives with three druids. The goddess Brigit was born in a druid's household; and Finn was reared by a druidess. The Ulster king Conchobar had a druid, Cathbadh, who enjoyed great influence. The druids were involved in the kingship ritual of the *tarbhfhess* (page 62). These Irish druids had a strong divinatory role: Cathbadh's prediction of Deirdre's disastrous effect upon Ulster (page 39) is an example. The ninth-century glossator Cormac comments on a divination ritual known as 'Himbas Forosnai', which involved chewing the raw flesh of pigs, dogs or cats. The Irish druids were also probably associated with the imposition of *geissi*, which were taboos or bonds placed upon prominent people and which they had to obey or perish.

Both Classical and Irish sources mention three religious and learned classes: the druids, bards and seers. Strabo alludes to the bards as being associated particularly with poetry; Irish bards were praise poets and involved with ceremonies related to Otherworld feasting; Finnegas the Bard was the means by which Finn gained knowledge from the Salmon of Wisdom. The seers (*vates* in Latin, *filidh* in Irish) were prominent in Ireland, where they had a function at least partly religious. They were responsible for the upkeep and transmission of sacred oral tradition. They were prophets and closely linked with divination, and they had the power to blemish or cause death by satire. Long after Ireland adopted Christianity, the *filidh* remained as seers, teachers and advisers, taking over many of the druids' functions. Indeed the *filidh* maintained a function until the seventeenth century. Brigit was the patron goddess of seers; she was perceived as expert in divination, prophecy, learning and poetry.

## Sacred space: groves, sanctuaries and pits

The axe-men came on an ancient and sacred grove. Its interlacing branches enclosed a cool central space into which the sun never shone, but where an abundance of water spouted from dark springs ... the barbaric gods worshipped here had their altars heaped with hideous offerings, and every tree was sprinkled with human blood ... Nobody dared enter this grove except the priest; and even he kept out at midday, and between dawn and dusk – for fear that the gods might be abroad at such hours.
(Lucan, *Pharsalia*, trans. Robert Graves, Penguin, 1956)

Thus Lucan describes a sacred Celtic grove near Marseille, felled by Caesar's army in the first century BC. The Celts' perception of numinosity, the presence of spirits, in all natural things (see 'Fertility, land and water', page 50) gave rise to the open-air worship of these beings. Groves were important partly because of the sanctity of individual trees and perhaps also because they were dark, mysterious and secret. While there can be no archaeological evidence for sacred groves or forests, there is abundant Classical literary reference to such places: Tacitus alludes to a druidic grove on Anglesey; Strabo speaks of Drunemeton, a holy grove of the Celtic Galatians in Asia Minor; and there are many more.

Some sacred space was demarcated from the profane world simply by means of a symbolic barrier which enclosed the numinous area. A piece of ground was designated as holy and thus a focus of communication with the supernatural world. The Goloring in Germany was a huge enclosure built in the sixth century BC; at its centre was an enormous wooden post, 40 feet (12 metres) high, perhaps symbolic of a sacred tree. Libenice in Czechoslovakia, dating to the fourth century BC, was a great, sub-rectangular enclosure which contained a sunken, unroofed structure at one end. Inside this 'shrine' were the remains of two timbers associated with two bronze torcs, perhaps once crude wooden statues of deities wearing Celtic symbols of prestige. Libenice contained sacrificial deposits of animals and the body of a woman, possibly the priestess of the sanctuary. Successive pits had been dug in the floor of the sunken structure over a period of twenty-four years, attesting the activity associated with some form of cult-ceremony.

Another group of open sacred sites were the *Viereckschanzen*, evidence of which has been found particularly in central Europe. They comprise square enclosures within which may be one or more ritual shafts. A *Viereckschanze* at Fellbach Schmiden near Stuttgart is interesting because of the discovery, inside the shaft, of oak animal-carvings, dated by dendrochronology (tree-ring dating) to the late second century BC. Ritual activity associated with pits may be interpreted as a means of associating with the infernal gods (see 'Death, rebirth and the Otherworld', page 76). Pits are certainly a recognisable category of sacred space: the Hampshire hillfort of Danebury has yielded abundant evidence of ritual behaviour associated with grain storage pits. Bodies of animals and humans (as well as other offerings) were interred in these pits, presumably as a means of communicating with and propitiating supernatural powers.

Built shrines were used by Iron Age Celts but there seem to have been no formalised religious structures such as existed in the Classical world. It is therefore often difficult to distinguish a temple from a house, and it is necessary to look for evidence of associated ritual activity in order to identify a sacred building as such. Sometimes the religious identity of a Celtic sanctuary is implied by the presence of an overlying Roman temple. Gournay (Oise) in France, was the site of an *oppidum* (urban settlement) of the Bellovaci, which contained an important pre-Roman sanctuary with complex associated ritual. The focus of the shrine in the third century BC was a great central pit in which the sacrificed bodies of elderly oxen were placed for decomposition before the bones were carefully positioned in the ditch surrounding the precinct. Young pigs and lambs were slaughtered and consumed in religious feasting; and 2000 weapons, ritually broken, were offered to the gods. The late Iron Age (first century BC) sanctuary at Hayling Island, Hampshire, consisted of a circular timber building surrounded by a courtyard which produced evidence for ritual, including ritually 'killed' weapons and the remains of sacrificed animals, with cattle apparently deliberately avoided, perhaps because of some local taboo. The identity of a rectangular porched shrine at South Cadbury hillfort in Somerset is suggested by the avenue of young animal-burials which led to it. In Ireland the great round structure at Navan (Co. Armagh) is undoubtedly a ritual monument. It had a huge central post, dendro-dated to 95/94 BC (when felled). Soon after it was built, the structure was deliberately burned down and sealed beneath a great stone cairn.

## Sacrifice and votive offerings

A sacrifice is the gift of something which is of value to the giver. The Celts made offerings to the gods of precious objects: these could be inanimate (tools or weapons, for instance), animals or – occasionally – humans. The more valuable the offering, the more powerful the act of propitiation: thus one would

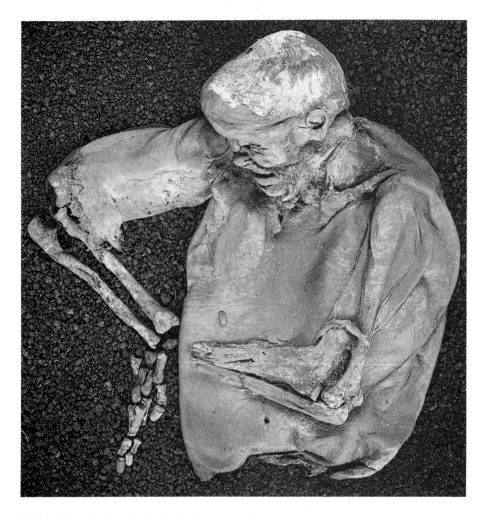

*Lindow Man: the Iron Age body found in a peat-bog at Lindow Moss, Cheshire.*

expect a human sacrifice to take place only at times of great need or to express great gratitude to the supernatural forces.

Although Classical sources make much of human sacrifice, there is little archaeological evidence to support the practice of ritual murder: Lucan and Tacitus tell of human remains heaped upon altars in sacred groves; there are reports of the imprisonment of malefactors for five years after which they were killed by being impaled; victims were stabbed, hanged, shot with arrows, or burned to death in huge wicker men. In examining the material evidence, care must be taken to distinguish genuine human sacrifice from bodies which were subjected to ritual after natural death. There is little unequivocal evidence for human sacrifice in the archaeological record of Celtic Europe. However, in a few instances, this manner of death does seem indicated. A clear example is Lindow Man, a young male of Iron Age date (first century AD), who suffered severe blows to his head, was garotted and had his throat cut before being thrust

*Bronze ceremonial shield, deposited as a votive gift in the river Thames at Battersea, London, in the first century BC. The shield was too fragile ever to have been used in battle, and it may have been made deliberately as an offering to the gods.*

face-down in a shallow pool in Lindow Moss, Cheshire. The young man was naked but for an armlet of fox-fur, and his body was painted. Just before he died, he ate what may have been a ritual meal, consisting of a wholemeal bread made of many different species of cereal grain and seed. There is very little allusion to human sacrifice in the vernacular sources, but one Irish tradition involved the ritual triple killing of a king, by burning, wounding and drowning, at the feast of Samhain.

Although animal-sacrifice is taken for granted as endemic in antiquity, it is important to understand the different forms such activity may take. Animals were often butchered and the meat shared between the community and the gods: some parts (usually the best cuts) were consumed and the rest buried or burnt as offerings. The other main type of sacrifice, that of an entire animal which was interred or burned (a holocaust), represented a considerable economic loss to the sacrificers since it involved taking a valuable sheep, pig or ox out

*Group of ritually-bent miniature spears (above) from the Romano-Celtic temple at Woodeaton, Oxfordshire.*

*Stone severed head (left) from a Romano-British shrine at Caerwent, South Wales.*

of productive circulation. Both kinds of sacrifice occurred at Gournay: oxen and horses were killed and left as offerings; piglets and lambs were eaten. At Danebury, Hampshire, animals were sometimes killed and interred as multiple burials in old grain storage pits. In Celtic cemeteries there is evidence both of ritual feasting on animals and of meat-offerings left to accompany the dead to the Otherworld. An interesting fact about Celtic animal sacrifice is that the vast majority of ritually slaughtered beasts belonged to domestic species.

## Votive offerings

Two aspects of votive offerings of inanimate objects are of especial interest: one is deposition in watery places; the other is ritual breakage. Both rituals were practised in Europe long before the main Celtic period. Both appear to have involved the separation of votive gifts from the mundane world by ritual 'killing', rendering them inaccessible or useless to humankind and thus appropriate gifts to the supernatural powers. At Flag Fen, Cambridgeshire, ritual deposits of metalwork, much of it deliberately broken, were made in the watery fen edge over a period between 1200 and 200 BC. Bent weapons were cast into the holy lake of Llyn Cerrig Bach (Anglesey) in the first century AD. The Gaulish sanctuary of Gournay produced hundreds of destroyed weapons. The Celtic healing goddess Sulis received thousands of Roman coins as gifts, placed in the great reservoir at Bath; many of these coins had been clipped to make them worthless as money. Some of the miniature weapons which were offered in Celtic shrines were snapped or bent in half: Harlow produced a group of four model iron daggers of which two had been broken before deposition.

## Rites of the human head

That head-hunting formed part of the cultic tradition of certain Celts is shown by archaeology, the Classical sources and the vernacular literature. Livy, Strabo and Diodorus all describe the decapitation of war victims, whose heads were either kept as trophies or offered in shrines. In the Celto-Ligurian area of southern Gaul, around Marseille, a distinctive group of pre-Roman sanctuaries and *oppida* attest the practice of ritual head-hunting. Most important of these is the cliff-top shrine of Roquepertuse (sixth–second century BC), the portico of which was adorned with niches containing the nailed-in skulls of young men who had died in battle. In Britain, at hillforts such as Bredon Hill (Worcestershire) heads mounted on poles guarded the entrances as symbolic protection for the strongholds. In late Romano-Celtic Britain, especially during the third and fourth centuries AD, certain individuals were decapitated after death before being interred in their tombs. Particularly curious rites took place around Kimmeridge in Dorset, where the bodies of old women were beheaded and the lower jaws removed. It is tempting to see these ladies as witches, prevented from talking and casting spells beyond the grave. That the human head was important in Celtic ritual is demonstrated by the emphasis on the head in Romano-Celtic iconography.

Heads play a prominent role in Welsh and Irish myth. The Ulster hero Cú Chulainn is said to have collected the heads of his enemies and placed them on stones. Two tales demonstrate the western Celts' perception of the magical properties of severed heads, particularly those of superhuman heroes. It was prophesied that the Ulstermen, smitten by Macha's curse of weakness, would regain their strength if they drank milk from the huge severed head of Conall Cernach. In this tale the head attains the properties of a cauldron of regeneration. Readers will recall the similar story of Bendigeidfran in the *Mabinogi*, whose severed head can speak and encourage his companions, bringing them good fortune on their long journey from Harlech to London.

# Death, rebirth and the Otherworld

That the Celts had a very profound and positive attitude to death is demonstrated by both literary and archaeological evidence. Julius Caesar comments that the Gauls believed in an ancestor-god, whom he identified with Dispater, the Roman god of the dead.

## The transmigration of souls

The druids attach particular importance to the belief that the soul does not perish but passes after death from one body to another.
(trans. Wiseman and Wiseman, 1980)

Caesar, commenting upon druidic doctrine, adds the acid remark that the druids promoted this idea in order that Gaulish warriors would not be afraid of death. Writing in the first century AD, Roman poet Lucan observes that the Celts regarded death merely as an interruption in a long life, as a stage between one life and another. Diodorus Siculus remarks that the Celts perceived men's souls to be immortal and that after a number of years people lived again, their souls inhabiting a new body. So there seems to have been a particular Celtic attitude to death which was discerned by contemporary observers from the Mediterranean world, an attitude which involved a kind of rebirth. The concept of souls living within a succession of bodies is similar to the picture of the Underworld painted by Virgil in the *Aeneid*.

## Perceptions of the Otherworld

The mythological traditions of the vernacular literature project the image of the Celtic Otherworld, to which humans passed after death, as an ambiguous place. Much is told about the Happy Otherworld, where the dead live again in a world very much like that of earth but better. Here there is neither pain, disease, ageing nor decay; it is a world full of music, feasting and beauty, though there is still combat between heroes. The other aspect of the Otherworld presents a sharp contrast: it can be a sombre place and full of danger, especially if visited by humans before death. As we saw in an earlier chapter, the Welsh Otherworld was called Annwn or Annwfn, and was described as a court of intoxication. Pwyll, lord of Dyfed, lives in Annwn for a year:

Of all the courts he had seen on earth, that was the court best furnished with meat and drink and vessels of gold and royal jewels.
(trans. Jones and Jones, 1976)

Other documents give more detail of Annwn. The *Spoils of Annwn* describes a magical cauldron, the typical Otherworld vessel of regeneration. It is a great, diamond-studded cauldron, boiled by the breath of nine virgins – perhaps evocative of fertility because of their untapped femininity, like Math's foot-holder (page 33). The Cauldron of Annwn refuses to cook food for a coward. The ambiguity of Annwn is expressed by the description of the Cwn Annwn (the Hounds of Annwn). In the *Mabinogi*, they are white with red ears – a colouring associated with the Otherworld. Another source speaks of the Cwn Annwn as hell-hounds, small, speckled, greyish-red beasts, chained and led by a black, horned figure. They are death-omens, sent from Annwn to seek out human souls. There is a sinister inexorability about these messengers of death which belies the carefree, happy image of the afterlife.

The Irish Otherworld is in many respects similar to Annwn. In Irish tradition the location of the supernatural world was variable: it could be perceived as on islands in the western ocean, beneath the sea or underground. Mounds called *sídhe* were the dwellings of the dispossessed Tuatha Dé Danann, allotted to each god by the Dagdha: each god had his own *sídh*, his Otherworld over which he presided. Another perception of the Irish Otherworld is as the hostel or *bruidhen* which could be situated in the countryside. The supernatural world could be reached by different means: by boat across the sea, as in the *Voyage of Bran*; entry could be gained by a lake or a cave. One entrance to the Otherworld was through the Lake of Cruachain.

In Irish myth the Otherworld is a timeless, ageless, happy place, a source of all wisdom, peace, beauty, harmony and immortality. Known as Tir na n'Og (the 'Land of Forever Young'), it is a world full of magic, enchantment and music. It is a place perceived as an idealised mirror-image of the human world. A feature of each *sídh* or hostel is the feast, central to which is the inexhaustible cauldron, always full of meat. A powerful image is that of the ever-renewing pig of the feast, slaughtered each day by the presiding god, and eternally reborn to be killed afresh the next day. The divine lord of the feast is frequently represented as a man with a pig slung over his shoulder.

Earthly time has no relevance in the Otherworld. If live humans visit it, they remain young while there, but should they return home, their earthly age will catch up with them. There are horrifying stories which describe the fate of people who come back from the supernatural world: Finn's son Oisin instantly ages 300 years when he returns and the same occurrence is recorded in the seventh-century *Voyage of Bran*. Bran and his men travel to the island called the Land of Women, a manifestation of the Happy Otherworld, where they stay for a time, but then some of the men become impatient for their homeland. Like Oisin they are warned not to touch the land but, as the boat approaches the Irish shore, one man leaps into the sea and flings himself on to the beach, only to crumble to dust.

A curious feature of the Celtic Otherworld is that supernatural beings sometimes have need of humans for activities they cannot perform themselves. Thus Pwyll is required by Arawn to fight Hafgan; Cú Chulainn fights battles for Otherworld beings; Finn is lured to the Otherworld by means of enchanted stags, boars, youths or women.

The sombre aspect of the Otherworld is equally represented in myth. Samhain, at the beginning of November, is a dangerous time, a kind of limbo where the barriers between the real and supernatural worlds are temporarily dissolved, and where humans and spirits can penetrate each other's space, thus upsetting the normal balance. As a land of the dead, the Otherworld can be dark and frightening. The Irish death-god Donn is a sombre being; Arawn, too, has a dark side, and Annwn can be dangerous. Thus in the *Spoils of Annwn*, Arthur barely escapes with his life after his quest for the magical cauldron. It seems that if humans visit the Otherworld while still alive, they are in danger. Thus Cú Chulainn sees all kinds of fearsome monsters and horrific visions. The tale of Da Derga's Hostel describes the *bruidhen* of a god wherein awaits the doom of the Irish king Conaire. On his way there Conaire encounters sinister harbingers of death, three red-clothed horsemen on red horses, their colour indicating their supernatural origin. He also sees the Irish goddess of destruction, the Badbh, who appears in triadic form, as three hideous black hags, naked and bleeding, with ropes around their necks. The symbolism of death, perhaps even human sacrifice, is intense here. Derga is a god of the dead, but the word can also refer to 'red', as if reflective of blood and death. The Badbh is a black, crow-like goddess and black is death's colour.

# Death

Archaeological findings suggest that the Iron Age Celts held certain beliefs associated with death and there is evidence of rituals and attempts to communicate with the infernal powers. The contents of graves may indicate a ritual which suggests the expectation of an afterlife. The placing of grave-goods with a body may imply a belief that the deceased would need them, or it might suggest rites of passage, a symbolic act of parting. Individuals of high status in early Iron Age France and Germany (seventh–sixth centuries BC) were buried under great mounds, with wagons and rich grave-furniture indicative of feasting: at Hochdorf in Germany, in the sixth century BC, a prince was laid on a bronze couch, accompanied by his cart, a vessel capable of holding 704 pints (400 litres) of mead and several drinking-horns. In later Iron Age Gaul and parts of Britain, high-ranking people were interred with two-wheeled chariots, weapons and feasting paraphernalia, including great joints of pork. Many graves demonstrate the perception of the funerary or Otherworld feast, with meat and drinking-vessels. Some very late Iron Age graves, dating from the late first century BC or early first century AD, in south-east Britain and on the Continent show the importance of feasting-rituals: amphorae, wine cups, firedogs to guard the cooking fire and meat are all present. It is tempting to link this banquet

*Iron Age burial of a warrior accompanied by his dismantled chariot, weapons and other grave-goods, from Somme-Bionne, France. It may have been believed that the dead man would need his sword and spears in the next world.*

*Chalk figurine of an infernal deity, from what may have been an underground shrine deep in a ritual pit at Deal, Kent. Second century AD.*

equipment with the Otherworld feast so dear to mythical perceptions of the Celtic afterlife.

While some sepulchral evidence displays the presence of formal Iron Age burial, it is clear that many people were not interred at death and, in Britain, graves are in fact relatively rare. Probably excarnation rituals were practised, whereby the body was exposed until it had decomposed and the spirit was thought to have left the body. Once the soul had departed, the bones could be disposed of without ceremony.

Communication with the infernal forces, assumed to dwell underground, was effected in various ways. At Danebury a particular ritual centred around disused corn-storage pits. Deposits of humans, parts of humans, animals or other offerings were placed at the bottom of these pits, which were then filled. These have been interpreted as thank-offerings to the Underworld gods whose space had been violated by the digging of the pits and who needed both to be placated and thanked for keeping the stored corn fresh.

Many areas of Britain and Celtic Europe show evidence of ritual pits and wells, whose main function may have been to communicate with the Underworld, propitiating the gods with sacrifices and votive gifts. At the Gournay sanctuary the focus of ritual activity was a huge central pit in which the bodies of sacrificed cattle were allowed to rot and feed the chthonic gods.

Links with the Underworld seem often to have been associated with dogs, which may have been symbols of death partly because of their hunting and scavenging imagery. The bodies of several dogs were buried in a deep pit at the shrine of Muntham Court in Sussex; five dog skulls were placed in a pit at Caerwent in Gwent. Some of the Danebury pits contained dogs, and there are many other such instances. That dogs had a mythic association with the Otherworld is demonstrated by the Cwn Annwn, the death-hounds of the Welsh Underworld.

## Images of rebirth

The most powerful symbol of regeneration, as projected in both the Welsh and the Irish myths, is the 'Cauldron of Rebirth'. The *bruidhen* or Otherworld hostel, furnished with its ever-replenishing cauldron, has already been discussed. The Irish god particularly associated with this symbol is the Dagdha. In the Welsh tale of Branwen, Bendigeidfran's Irish magic cauldron is described: it can restore dead warriors to life, if they are cooked in it overnight. The soldiers rise again as strong as before, but they have lost the power of speech – a sure sign that they are still dead. This regenerative potency is paralleled by the healing well of the Irish divine leech, Dian Cécht, who restores dead warriors to life by immersing them in the water and chanting incantations over them. Interestingly one of the inner plates of the Gundestrup Cauldron perhaps displays the resurrective properties of cauldrons: it shows a large supernatural figure with a group of Celtic soldiers, one of whom the god is either dipping into or removing from a large vat of liquid.

*Late Iron Age cremation grave of a British aristocrat, with equipment for the funerary feast, from Welwyn, Hertfordshire.*

Clearly both the vessel and the liquid possess healing, restorative powers in the vernacular myths. Archaeological evidence supports this association between cauldrons and water-ritual: ceremonial cauldrons of sheet-bronze were used as early as the Bronze Age. In the Celtic Iron Age many great cult cauldrons are recorded: the vessels at Llyn Fawr and Llyn Cerrig in Wales; Brå, Rynkeby and Gundestrup in Denmark; Duchcov in Czechoslovakia were all associated with lakes or springs.

Rebirth could be symbolised by other vessels and liquids. In Romano-Celtic iconography, especially in Burgundy, the Gaulish hammer-god is depicted with wine barrels and goblets of red wine which seem to have been symbols of resurrection. An interesting aspect of Celtic perceptions about death and rebirth, associated with blood, is expressed in the imagery of the divine hunt, which is present in many of the myths. Since hunting required bloodshed in order to provide nourishment, the act of hunting acquired the symbolism of resurrection, and the interdependent dualism which exists between life and death. The wine-symbolism of the Burgundian iconography may likewise be linked with blood, death and rebirth.

Certain creatures are particularly symbolic of renewal: the snake was a potent image of rebirth, and the association of this reptile with both death and fertility has already been noted (page 58). Birds, with their power to leave earth in flight, naturally became identified with the perception of the spirit rising free from the body at death, an idea which persisted into medieval Christian symbolism. Otherworld deities are often associated with birds: the Irish Clíodna had three magical birds which could heal with their song; the three singing birds of Rhiannon, alluded to in the *Mabinogi*, express the same perception of birds that symbolise life after death. Stags possessed regenerative imagery, probably because of the seasonal shedding and regrowth of their antlers, which evoked the symbolism of autumn and spring.

Trees were important symbols of rebirth. Deciduous trees apparently died in winter, their bare branches silhouetted against the sky like the bones of a skeleton, but in spring they were born again, producing new leaves and then fruit. Trees were also seen as a link between life and death, the upper and lower worlds, with their branches stretching towards the sky and their roots buried deep underground. It is interesting that trees, particularly apple trees, feature in many Otherworld myths. Clíodna's birds eat fruit from the sacred apple tree; in the *Voyage of Bran* the symbol of the Otherworld goddess is an apple branch, silver with white blossom. The Happy Otherworld of Arthurian Romance is Avalon, the Paradise of Apple Trees, a magical island in the West.

*The god Esus chopping down a willow, perhaps the Tree of Life, from Nôtre Dame, Paris, France. Early first century AD.*

# Suggestions for further reading

A number of general reference books on the ancient Celts is available: T. G. E. Powell, *The Celts* (London, 1958, with numerous reprints); B. Cunliffe, *The Celtic World* (London, 1979, 1992), provides a well-illustrated overview; N. Chadwick, *The Celts* (Penguin, 1970). For those wishing to gain detailed, up-to-date information on the archaeology of the Celts, the lavishly illustrated and well-researched catalogue of the 1991 Venice Exhibition (*The Celts*, London, 1991) is good value (available in hardback and paperback).

The vernacular myths of Ireland and Wales exist in translation in various editions. One of the best collections of Welsh myths is G. and T. Jones, *The Mabinogion* (London, 1976). The Irish material is more scattered: T. Kinsella, *The Táin* (Dublin, 1969), and C. O'Rahilly, *Táin Bó Cuailnge* (Dublin, 1970), present the main Ulster Cycle myths. For the Tuatha Dé Danann see H. D'Arbois de Jubainville, *The Mythological Cycle* (Dublin, 1903); T. F. O'Rahilly, *Early Irish History and Mythology* (Dublin, 1946). Other useful sources on Ireland include P. Mac Cana, *Celtic Mythology* (London, 1983); D. Ó'Hógain, *The Encyclopaedia of Irish Folklore, Legend and Romance* (London, 1991); T. P. Cross and C. H. Slover, *Ancient Irish Tales* (London, 1937); M. Dillon, *Early Irish Literature* (Chicago, 1948); J. Gantz, *Early Irish Myths and Sagas* (Penguin, 1981). For discussion of Welsh and Irish myths and their relationship to archaeological evidence see M-L. Sjoestedt, *Gods and Heroes of the Celts* (Berkeley, 1982); A. and B. Rees, *Celtic Heritage* (London, 1961); M. J. Green, *Dictionary of Celtic Myth and Legend* (London, 1992).

For general archaeological background to Iron Age Celts in Britain see B. Cunliffe, *Iron Age Communities in Britain* (London, 1991). For an examination of the relationship between Celts and Indo-Europeans, J. B. Mallory, *In Search of the Indo-Europeans* (London, 1989), is probably the most sensible source. For sanctuaries and ritual see S. Piggott, *The Druids* (London, 1968, with reprints); J-L. Brunaux, *The Celtic Gauls: Gods, Rites and Sanctuaries* (London, 1988); A. Woodward, *Shrines and Sacrifice* (London, 1992); G. A. Wait, *Ritual and Religion in Iron Age Britain* (British Archaeological Reports, Oxford, 1985); I. M. Stead, *Lindow Man: The Body in the Bog* (London, 1986). For Iron Age art see R. and V. Megaw, *Celtic Art from its beginnings to the Book of Kells* (London, 1989). For religion and the gods see H. E. Davidson, *Myths and Symbols in Pagan Europe* (Manchester, 1988), which explores the relationship between Celtic and Norse religion and myth; M. J. Green, *The Gods of the Celts* (Gloucester, 1986), *Symbol and Image in Celtic Religious Art* (London, 1989, 1992) and *Animals in Celtic Life and Myth* (London, 1992); A. Ross, *Pagan Celtic Britain* (London, 1967) and *The Pagan Celts* (London, 1986). Good surveys in French include P-M. Duval, *Les Dieux de la Gaule* (Paris, 1976); J. de Vries, *La Religion des Celtes* (Paris, 1963); E. Thevenot, *Divinités et sanctuaires de la Gaule* (Paris, 1968).

# Index